Contents

ANA's Legislative and Regulatory Initiatives by Major Category

LEGISLATIVE
— AND —
REGULATORY INITIATIVES
— FOR THE —
106TH CONGRESS

ANA

**AMERICAN NURSES
ASSOCIATION**

Department of Government Affairs

AMERICAN NURSES ASSOCIATION

Department of Government Affairs
Phone: (202) 651-7081
Fax: (202) 554-0189

Marjorie W. Vanderbilt (651-7085)	Director
Sheila Abood, MS, RN (651-7093)	Associate Director
K. Reeder Franklin (651-7097)	Associate Director
Rose Gonzalez, MPS, RN (651-7098)	Associate Director
Jacqueline Pomfret (651-7099)	Associate Director
Stephanie Reed (651-7088)	Associate Director
Jocelyn E. Coffey (651-7083)	Senior Administrative Assistant
Doretta Hood (651-7094)	Senior Administrative Assistant
Mary Marra (651-7092)	Senior Political Action Specialist
Sheila Roit, MPP, RN (651-7090)	Senior Political Action Specialist
Anne Berry (651-7096)	ANA-PAC Coordinator
Sylvia Thomas (651-7082)	Administrative Assistant

Published by
American Nurses Publishing
600 Maryland Avenue, SW
Suite 100 West
Washington, DC 20024-2571

ISBN 1-55810-145-4

9904LR   4M   09/99

Introduction

The American Nurses Association (ANA) is the only full-service professional organization representing the nation's entire registered nurse (RN) population. From the halls of Congress and federal agencies to boardrooms, hospitals, and other health care facilities, ANA is the strongest voice for the nursing profession and for workplace advocacy. It is headquartered in Washington, D.C.

ANA represents the interests of the nation's 2.6 million RNs through its 53 constituent state and territorial associations. More than 25 of ANA's constituent associations serve as collective bargaining agents for nurses. ANA is a professional association for nurses as well as the strongest labor union for the nursing profession.

One unique purpose of ANA is to shape public policy about health care to be consonant with the goals of nurses, nursing, and public health. ANA's House of Delegates establishes policies and goals for the profession that form the basis for nursing's contribution to the advancement of health care policy. These goals serve as the foundation for a variety of ANA program activities. Among these activities are ANA's legislative efforts: ANA seeks enactment and implementation of legislation that will benefit the health and welfare of the nation's citizens.

Decisions affecting public policy about health care are made at the national, state, and local levels. Although the policies and goals put forth by ANA's House of Delegates guide this process for the profession, it is recognized that health care policy for the people is determined by legislative bodies as they adopt laws, executive bodies as they administer laws, and judicial bodies as they interpret laws.

ANA's legislative and regulatory agenda is comprehensive and encompasses nursing education, nursing practice, research, collective bargaining, workplace advocacy, and federal regulation. ANA has been at the forefront of advocating for access to quality health care services for all individuals and is committed to ensuring that the RN is an essential provider in all practice settings.

Each year, specific legislative priorities are adopted by ANA and shared with nurses and policymakers. This publication outlines ANA's legislative and regulatory priorities for the 106th Congress. We hope you find this publication a useful tool as critical health care issues are considered.

Background

ANA Goals and Positions on Legislative and Regulatory Initiatives for the 106th Congress

The legislative and regulatory initiatives described here are derived from goals adopted by the American Nurses Association (ANA) 1997 House of Delegates. They are intended to serve as a guide for ANA and state nurses association (SNA) interactions with the U.S. Congress and federal agencies. These initiatives focus on a combination of ANA's program activities and its goals for the nursing profession.

GOAL

I

NURSE ADVOCACY

ANA and SNAs will ensure that the registered nurse is an essential provider in all practice settings through education, research, collective bargaining, workplace advocacy, legislation, and regulation.

LEGISLATIVE

Legislative efforts on workforce issues will focus on defining and enacting measures to ensure patient safety and quality care through appropriate nursing care in all appropriate settings by adequate numbers of well-prepared nurses.

Specific legislative actions include the following:

- Promote patient care legislation that includes required reporting of nurse staffing levels and mix at health care institutions, whistle-blower protection for nurses who report unsafe patient care, and a mechanism to ensure that community health needs will be met before institutional mergers and acquisitions are approved.

- Promote changes to the National Labor Relations Act (NLRA) to support collective bargaining in the health care workplace and clarify the status of registered nurses (RNs) as employees.

- Promote initiatives that provide funding for existing hospital staff to participate in retraining programs in anticipation of the future health care workplace.

- Strengthen collective bargaining by opposing legislation that would compromise the independence of collective bargaining units from management and would revise wage-and-hour laws without strong protection for workers from coercive practices that could erode the 40-hour work week.

- Support legislation to bar permanent replacement of striking workers and to prohibit discrimination against those who participate in strikes.

- Support adequate funding for the Occupational Safety and Health Administration (OSHA) within the Department of Labor and the National Institute of Occupational Safety and Health (NIOSH) within the Department of Health and Human Services (DHHS). ANA will also oppose inappropriate political and congressional interference in the research and enforcement responsibilities of these agencies.

- Support efforts to maintain and strengthen the Social Security system.

REGULATORY

- Promote the National Labor Relations Board's (NLRB's) authority to engage in rule-making on appropriate bargaining units in health care.
- Maintain an ongoing relationship with the Department of Labor (DOL) on workforce issues affecting nurses.
- Advocate for a strong and adequately staffed Office of Occupational Health Nursing within OSHA.
- Promote agency research and regulatory activity on occupational health and safety, especially on the impact of restructuring on the health and safety of nurses.
- Monitor and make recommendations on DOL and Immigration and Naturalization Service (INS) activities on immigration issues that affect nurses.
- Work with DHHS to implement broad use of the ANA-developed report card to measure quality indicators and outcomes in relation to nurse staffing issues.
- Monitor court actions as they relate to the collective bargaining rights of nurses.
- Monitor actions of OSHA and DOL as they relate to workplace violence.
- Enhance collective bargaining efforts in the Department of Veterans Affairs (DVA).
- Monitor restructuring initiatives involving the nursing workforce in federal agencies, including DVA and the Indian Health Service (IHS).
- Support data collection, retraining, and education programs for nurses within DOL and DHHS to meet the future needs of the health care workforce.
- Support funding for health services research on patient outcomes, impact of nursing on the health care delivery system, and cost-effective nursing interventions.
- Work with the Agency for Health Care Policy and Research (AHCPR) on linking nursing interventions to quality of patient care.

GOAL

II ACCESS TO QUALITY HEALTH CARE

ANA and SNAs will collectively and collaboratively advocate for access to comprehensive quality health care services for all people.

LEGISLATIVE

In 1999–2000, ANA will work toward the passage of federal legislation that advances nursing's agenda for health care reform, with particular attention given to proposals that will move toward achieving 100 percent universal health care coverage for all citizens and residents, improving the quality and scope of current programs, and ensuring that quality of care considerations are given at least equal weight as cost in assessing both public and private health care plans.

Specific activities related to these health care issues include the following:

- Support Medicaid reimbursement for all advanced practice nurse (APNs) regardless of geographic location, practice setting, or category of APN and regardless of whether they are working under the supervision of or in association with a physician.

- Support funding for graduate nurse education that is not subject to the uncertainties of the annual appropriations process.

- Support adequate funding in the appropriations process for the Nurse Education Act (NEA) and the National Institute of Nursing Research (NINR).

- Ensure that both public and private health plans include coverage for nurse provider services and participation of nurses in the plans.

- Oppose antitrust measures that would enable any group of providers to achieve or maintain market dominance over any other group of providers.

- Oppose caps on noneconomic damages under malpractice reform.

- Advocate for nursing participation in health promotion and disease prevention legislative proposals, including provider reimbursement for clinical services.

- Support legislative approaches to decrease violence in society, including guns, domestic violence, violence against gays and lesbians, and violence in the workplace.

- Support programs that promote health services in rural areas and among other underserved populations, including appropriate use of telehealth.

- Support insurance reform initiatives that improve access to high-quality health care.

- Support legislation to protect full and open provider-patient communication and privacy.

- Oppose arbitrary limits on public or private coverage for and access to a full range of health services for prevention and treatment.

- Support long-term care proposals to improve access to home, community-based, and institutional care and for the use of sufficient numbers of qualified RNs in roles such as case managers.

- Support Medicare legislation that would conform the role of RNs in Medicare home health care in the areas of development of a beneficiary's plan of care and for certification and recertification of need to the law governing skilled nursing facilities.

- Support the development and continuation of innovative community health care models operated and staffed by RNs.

- Oppose arbitrary, budget-driven cuts in the Medicare and Medicaid programs.

- Oppose mandatory human immunodeficiency virus (HIV) testing and mandatory disclosure of HIV status of patients and nurses.

- Oppose any initiative that restricts nonemergency health care, public health, and education services to undocumented aliens.

- Support efforts to ensure that a patient's basic right to privacy is protected.

- Improve access to high-quality effective pain and symptom management and palliative care in order to ensure that the needs of chronic pain patients and those who are terminally ill are met.

REGULATORY

- Monitor and promote nursing to the Medicare Payment Advisory Commission (MedPAC) by focusing attention on its provider payment reform issues and provider education issues.

- Respond to proposed changes in prospective payment system (PPS) regulations that affect nursing payment.
- Support the implementation of regulations to achieve payment for nursing services, regardless of site or setting, through Medicare, Medicaid, Federal Employees Health Benefits Plan, and the Civilian Health and Medical Programs of the United States (CHAMPUS).
- Support appropriate standards and guidelines regarding encroachment on professional nursing practice in federal health systems.
- Monitor implementation of federal initiatives that fund nursing education programs under NEA, National Health Service Corps, Office of Minority Health, IHS, Department of Defense (DOD), DVA, and Department of Agriculture.
- Support data collection from a variety of sources concerning the future demand for nursing as it relates to the total health care workforce. Monitor and support, as appropriate, the activities of the Division of Nursing (DON), DHHS. Monitor the activities of the Council on Graduate Medical Education (COGME) and the Institute of Medicine (IOM) that relate to nursing education.
- Support health promotion and disease prevention efforts of the U.S. Public Health Service (PHS).
- Work with the federal agencies that administer programs to increase access to quality care for vulnerable populations, including community and migrant health centers, rural health initiatives, programs assisting people with HIV and acquired immune deficiency syndrome (AIDS), and nutritional programs.
- Support the federal government's role and responsibility in regulating long-term care facilities, in areas such as the role of nursing, composition of survey teams, drug administration guidelines, criteria for resident assessment and facility definition, and patient restraints.
- Work with the Health Care Financing Administration (HCFA) to advocate the adoption of quality indicators and a nursing report card to link the quality of care to nursing interventions.
- Promote the appointment of nurses to federal advisory councils, boards, and commissions throughout the health policy and labor arenas.

GOAL
III

ANA/SNA VIABILITY
ANA and the SNAs as multipurpose organizations will continue to be strong and effective at the national and state levels.

Many federal legislative and regulatory activities relate directly to state governments and often depend on state implementation. ANA will work to ensure that SNAs have timely and useful information about such activities so that they will be able to work effectively at the state level to ensure that the nursing profession is heard. Among the activities are the following:

LEGISLATIVE

- Monitor federal proposals and court actions on state waiver programs, such as Medicaid and ERISA, that directly affect state health care reform efforts.

- Oppose federal legislative efforts to block grant health and welfare programs to the states without adequate funding or enforcement mechanisms or with inappropriate restrictions, which could hamper health care quality and access.
- Support legislative initiatives that promote and increase cultural diversity in the nursing profession, enhance nurses' awareness of cultural diversity issues, and improve the cultural competence of nurses in the delivery of health care.
- Enhance the political education and political action of nurses across the nation and monitor legislative initiatives, such as campaign finance reform and lobby disclosure proposals that affect those goals.
- Strengthen and enhance ANA's grassroots key contact and strength-in-numbers programs and coordinate these efforts with the SNAs by providing critical materials to individual nurses about the action of their federal legislators.

REGULATORY

- Monitor federal agency activities as they relate to waiver proposals from individual states to implement state health care reform.
- Promote development of special projects and initiatives for minorities and disadvantaged nursing students.
- Advocate for an increase in the number of nurses appointed to political positions.

ANA Department of Government Affairs

ANA's strength and success on Capitol Hill are due to the collaboration and coordination of three critical programs—lobbying, grassroots activities, and political action. These three programs are under the jurisdiction of the Department of Government Affairs. The success of nursing's legislative agenda is due to the fact that ANA has crafted and maintained well-rounded and complementary programs that effectively influence policymakers at all levels of government.

LEGISLATIVE AND REGULATORY PROGRAM

The Department of Government Affairs currently has five lobbyists who are experts in health care and workforce issues. It is their responsibility to educate members of Congress and their staffs about ANA's legislative and regulatory agenda. Each lobbyist monitors specific congressional committees and issues. In addition, the department has one regulatory specialist who works with the federal departments and agencies.

- ANA lobbyists are closely involved with legislative initiatives from conception through enactment. For example, ANA lobbyists often work with members of Congress to develop a legislative proposal that eventually is introduced as a bill. ANA lobbyists then encourage other members of Congress to co-sponsor the bill in a demonstration of support for the initiative. After the bill has been referred to a committee or subcommittee, ANA lobbyists work with the relevant congressional staff as the proposal is reviewed. Lobbyists often participate in the congressional hearing process by writing testimony and preparing an ANA official to testify before the committee or subcommittee.

- Inasmuch as broad-based bipartisan support is necessary to win approval of a legislative proposal, ANA lobbyists often form or join coalitions that consist of other nursing organizations, health care groups, labor unions, consumer groups, and women's and minority organizations to advocate for a specific proposal. When legislation moves to the entire Senate or House of Representatives for consideration, ANA lobbyists meet with individual members of Congress and their staffs to discuss ANA's position on the proposal. Because ANA lobbyists combine an expertise in specific health-related areas with an extensive knowledge of the workings of the Congress, they are able to effectively advance nursing's legislative agenda.

- ANA lobbyists coordinate their activities with ANA's political and grassroots staff to ensure that the Nurses Strategic Action Team (N-STAT), ANA's rapid response grassroots team, is activated when needed. ANA's Washington, D.C., lobbying team has had a significant and growing impact in Congress because of the combined efforts of the tens of thousands of nurses who participate in N-STAT, the hundreds of nurses who are committed to political and legislative action through their involvement in the N-STAT Leadership Team, and the SNAs that help to ensure that their members are informed and active.

- ANA lobbyists also work with the federal agencies that promulgate regulations after a bill has been enacted into law. ANA lobbyists work primarily with DHHS and its DON, NINR, HCFA, AHCPR, DOL, DVA, and DOD. In addition, ANA lobbyists work closely with numerous federal and congressional commissions.

- The staff of the Department of Government Affairs writes and edits *Capitol Update*, a biweekly newsletter that provides information on and analysis of current legislative, regulatory, and political issues. At the beginning of each new Congress, the department also prepares this publication, *Legislative and Regulatory Initiatives*, which details legislative and regulatory issues critical to nurses and health care consumers.

POLITICAL PROGRAM

ANA's Political Action Committee (ANA-PAC) and complementary political education programs are key to ANA's legislative success in Congress. The Department of Government Affairs currently has four senior political action specialists who are each responsible for all political and grassroots activities in one of four regions of the country (East, Midwest, South, and West). In addition, the department has an ANA-PAC coordinator who coordinates the political fund-raising and endorsement activities with the ANA-PAC Board of Trustees.

ANA-PAC not only raises money to contribute to candidates running for political office, but also increases nurses' participation in the political and legislative processes. More than 12,000 individual nurses currently contribute to ANA-PAC. In 1998 the average contribution was approximately $45.

The primary source of ANA-PAC funds is an integrated phone/mail campaign. In the 1993–1994, 1995–1996, and 1997–1998 election cycles, ANA-PAC raised more than $1 million to contribute to congressional candidates. ANA-PAC is the fourth largest health care PAC in the United States.

In each election cycle, every effort is made to ensure that each ANA-PAC-endorsed congressional candidate has contact with nurses in his or her state or district during the campaign. ANA-PAC support is obtained through several means, including direct financial contributions, paid radio and print media advertisements, volunteer campaign efforts, campaign polling, phone banks staffed on specified nights, candidate forums and debates, and house parties and "meet-and-greets" hosted to introduce candidates to local nurses.

To increase the political activism of nurses across the country and to encourage nurses to form working relationships with their elected officials in order to educate them about today's critical health care issues, in 1998 ANA designated October 14 as Nurses Campaign Activity Night 1998 (Nurses CAN '98). On that night ANA urged all nurses to volunteer on the campaign of their choice at the federal, state, or local level. Nurses CAN '98 was an enormous success across the country and will become a regular event sponsored by ANA each election year.

GRASSROOTS PROGRAM

ANA has been able to have a significant and growing impact in Congress mostly because of the tens of thousands of nurses who participate in N-STAT, ANA's grassroots lobbying program.

N-STAT was initiated in 1993 for nursing to have an impact on the health care reform debate. Since that time it has evolved into a very strong grassroots lobbying force. Approximately 40,000 nurses currently participate in N-STAT's grassroots mobilization efforts. These nurses constitute the N-STAT Rapid Response Team. When grassroots activity is needed on a specific legislative issue, the team can be called into action in a matter of hours.

The other component of N-STAT, the N-STAT Leadership Team (formerly known as Senate Coordinators and Congressional District Coordinators), is composed of individual nurses who establish an effective working relationship with their Senator(s) and/or Representative in Congress through political and grassroots activities. These individuals serve as key contacts with their respective Senator(s) and/or Representative and communicate with them on a regular basis. They often serve as a liaison between ANA's lobbyists and specific members of Congress on key issues. The nurses who make up the N-STAT Leadership Team also help organize legislative meetings, develop telephone trees for rapid response to legislative initiatives, and help coordinate campaign and election activities.

1

Access to Quality Health Care for All Patients

Community Nursing Organizations

ISSUE

Extension and expansion of the Community Nursing Organization (CNO) Demonstration Project.

BACKGROUND

The CNO Demonstration Project was authorized under the Omnibus Budget Reconciliation Act (OBRA) of 1987. Each CNO is a nurse-operated and -administered program serving Medicare beneficiaries in home- and community-based settings under contracts that provide a fixed monthly capitation payment for each beneficiary who elects to enroll. Similar in nature to health maintenance organizations (HMOs), CNOs agree to provide all Medicare Part B benefits (except physician, laboratory, and x-ray services), including home care services; physical, occupational and speech-hearing therapies; medical equipment and supplies; and ambulance services to enrollees for a single monthly payment. In addition, CNOs provide services such as case management, health education, and preventive services. The demonstration project was originally a three-year project. Actual delivery of health care services began in January 1994 and was scheduled to expire on December 31, 1996. The Health Care Financing Administration (HCFA) extended the project through December 31, 1997, and then an additional two-year extension (through December 31, 1999) was provided with passage of the Balanced Budget Act of 1997 (Public Law 105-33).

Four sites were selected for the demonstration project and are operating today:

- Carondelet Health Services, Inc., Tucson, Arizona;
- Carle Clinic Association, Urbana, Illinois;
- Living at Home Block Nurse Program, St. Paul, Minnesota; and
- Visiting Nurse Service of New York, Long Island City, New York.

ANA POSITION

During the 106th Congress, ANA will work to make permanent the authority for existing CNO sites to enroll and provide care to Medicare beneficiaries and to authorize the establishment of additional sites on a demonstration basis.

The continuation of the CNO demonstration project will not increase Medicare expenditures for care. CNOs save Medicare dollars by providing better and more accessible care in home and community settings, thereby allowing beneficiaries to avoid unnecessary hospitalization and nursing home admissions. By demonstrating what a primary care-oriented nursing practice can accomplish with patients who are elderly or disabled, CNOs help to show how to increase benefits, save money, and improve the quality of life for patients. ANA will continue to work closely with both the CNOs and members of the 106th Congress on the extension and expansion of CNO services for Medicare beneficiaries.

Emerging Majority

ISSUE

Access to health care for an ethnically and culturally diverse population.

BACKGROUND

The health needs of the emerging majority are a high priority for the nursing profession. Recent actions by its House of Delegates have enabled ANA to identify an organizational strategy that

■ Increases access to health care for minorities,

■ Increases access to education for minorities, and

■ Broadens ANA's and nursing's representation and work in minority communities.

In the 104th Congress there were several proposals at the federal and state levels (e.g., California's Proposition 187) that banned nonemergency health care and public health services to undocumented aliens. These provisions would have required nurses, physicians, and other health care providers to deny all health care, except emergency care, to anyone who merely is suspected of being an undocumented immigrant. In addition, several of the proposals would require health care providers to act as law enforcers by reporting such persons to the Immigration and Naturalization Service.

During the 105th Congress, President Clinton launched his "Initiative on Race." He pledged to eliminate the disparities in six areas of health status experienced by racial and ethnic minority populations by the year 2010. Eliminating racial and ethnic disparities in health care will require enhanced efforts in preventing disease, promoting health, and delivering appropriate care. ANA was present at the White House announcement of this initiative and is committed to working with the administration to achieve these goals.

ANA POSITION

ANA historically has opposed any public policy that unfairly discriminates. ANA is committed to the elimination of the dramatic disparities in the delivery of health care. ANA believes that access to preventive health care, nutritional programs, and educational opportunities will promote economic security and social empowerment. ANA considers any requests of nurses to deny services to those in need based on citizenship and any requirements that nurses "report" undocumented persons a compromise to the integrity of the profession and the practice of the individual nurse. ANA will pursue educational funding for health care workers to increase the number of professionals who are ethnically and culturally competent.

Federal Health Budget and Appropriations

ISSUE

Adequate funding for health programs in the face of continuing pressure to reduce the federal budget deficit.

BACKGROUND

The size of the federal budget deficit skyrocketed during the 1980s because of tax cuts, increases in defense spending, and recession. Federal debt in the 1980s grew from $1 trillion to more than $4 trillion. Continued budget deficits are damaging to the economy and pose potential problems for future generations. A number of mechanisms have been implemented during the last decade to force fiscal discipline on both the executive and legislative branches of the federal government. Although mechanisms have helped keep the deficit from rising faster than it might have, projections indicate that some sectors, especially in health care, will continue to rise faster than income.

The Balanced Budget Act of 1997 (Public Law 105-33) set caps on discretionary spending that provided a short-term boost in discretionary spending with increasingly tighter caps through 2002. Adjusted for inflation, discretionary spending faces an almost 10 percent cut. Unless the budget caps on discretionary spending are raised or evaded, they will require a $4 billion cut in outlays in fiscal year 2000. The fiscal year 1999 budget is expected to have a surplus of approximately $111 billion.

The dilemma for Congress and the administration remains. Should the surplus be returned to taxpayers via a tax cut, should Congress raise the tight "caps" on appropriations for military and domestic discretionary spending, or should the surplus be used to pay down a portion of the $5.5 trillion national debt? To compound these issues, by fiscal year 2014 the cost of Social Security benefits will start to exceed payroll revenues and by fiscal year 2032 this trust fund may be bankrupt. President Clinton has stated that nothing should be done with the overall budget surplus until agreement can be reached on a long-term solution that resolves the Social Security funding problem.

ANA POSITION

ANA recognizes the need to address the growing federal deficit by limiting the growth in expenditures. However, ANA believes that the path to deficit reduction must take into account the critical role federal funding plays in assuring quality health care for the nation. Within the domestic discretionary spending accounts funded through annual appropriations, ANA strongly supports current funding levels for programs that help provide an adequate supply of health professionals, including programs under the Nurse Education Act (NEA), the National Institute of Nursing Research (NINR), the Occupational Safety and Health Administration (OSHA), and the National Institute of Occupational Safety and Health (NIOSH). It is crucial that the nursing workforce be able to meet the needs of our rapidly changing health delivery system and that its members represent the economic and ethnic diversity of our nation.

Gun Control

ISSUE

Control of the purchase and use of firearms.

BACKGROUND

Former U.S. Surgeon General C. Everett Koop cited violence as a public health crisis. The number of Americans killed or wounded by handguns each year has reached epidemic proportions. Handgun Control, Inc., in Washington, D.C., cites the following:

■ In 1996, 10,744 people were murdered with firearms in this country.

■ In 1996, firearms were used in two of three murders committed in the United States.

■ In 1995, 14 children, ages 19 and under, were killed with guns every day in this country.

■ More than $1 billion is spent annually on hospital costs associated with the treatment of individuals who have been shot.

■ Firearm injuries total more than $14.4 billion in lifetime costs per year. Lifetime costs include medical costs and loss of productivity.

■ Although the federal government keeps no specific records on assault weapons, the Bureau of Alcohol, Tobacco, and Firearms (ATF) estimates that there are one million semiautomatic assault weapons in private hands in the United States.

■ Licensed firearms dealers sell an estimated 7.5 million guns every year, of which 3.5 million are handguns.

During the 103rd Congress, two major pieces of gun control legislation were enacted. One required a five-day waiting period for the purchase of handguns. The second banned the sale of certain semiautomatic assault weapons. Attempts to repeal those two laws during the 104th Congress were unsuccessful. Instead, during the 104th Congress several significant pieces of gun control legislation were enacted, including a bill to prevent domestic abusers from possessing firearms and a bill making it a federal crime to possess a gun within a school zone if the gun had crossed interstate lines. In the 105th Congress, ANA was a strong supporter of legislation to make it more difficult for children to gain access to guns, thereby preventing shootings in America's schools. This legislation will be reintroduced in the 106th Congress.

ANA POSITION

There is a definite need to control handgun use and the accompanying violence that leads individuals to use handguns. ANA believes that nurses can play a critical role in reducing gun-related violence by educating health care consumers about the dangers associated with gun ownership. ANA supports the waiting period for the purchase of handguns, a ban on the sale of all assault weapons, and other federal initiatives that work to decrease the many dangers associated with gun violence.

Health Care: An Overview

ISSUE

Access to quality health care for all U.S. citizens and residents.

BACKGROUND

Since the Clinton administration's comprehensive health reform efforts failed in 1994, many members of Congress have concentrated on incremental reforms to improve both access to and the quality of health care. The 105th Congress enacted major changes in the Medicare and Medicaid programs as part of the Balanced Budget Act of 1997 (Public Law 105-33). Those changes are having an impact on the delivery of care to significant numbers of Americans. Greater changes will occur when the regulations implementing provisions of Public Law 105-33 are promulgated.

Throughout the health care system, questions about quality and access of care have led to calls for more patient protections, especially in managed care settings. In institutional settings, the replacement of registered nurses (RNs) with unlicensed assistive personnel decreases the quality of care and threatens patient safety. Increases in the cost of health insurance coupled with decreases in employer support for employee benefits have led to a growth in the number of Americans without health insurance.

ANA POSITION

ANA supports a reformed health care system that ensures access, quality, and services at affordable costs. "Nursing's Agenda for Health Care Reform" calls for a

- Basic core of essential health care services to be available to everyone;
- Restructured health care system that focuses on consumers and their health, with services to be delivered in convenient sites by the most appropriate provider;
- Requirement to use all primary care providers, including nurse practitioners (NPs), clinical nurse specialists (CNSs), and certified nurse midwives (CNMs); and
- Shift from the predominant focus on illness and cure to an orientation toward wellness and care.

ANA believes that appropriate numbers of RNs, in current and reformed health care settings, are essential to maintaining the safety and quality of patient care. Restructuring plans by employers to decrease the use of RNs and increase the use of lower-paid, assistive personnel will prove to be a poor investment over the long term if the quality and safety of patient care are compromised to achieve short-term cost savings.

Building on the core principles of its Nursing's Agenda for Health Care Reform, ANA, in a managed care policy adopted in 1998, reiterated its support for policies that protect consumers, enhance accountability for quality, and promote access to the full range of health care services.

Malpractice (Tort) Reform

ISSUE

Reform of the medical malpractice system, balancing of the concerns of health care practitioners and the need for victims to be compensated for injury resulting from practitioner negligence.

BACKGROUND

In the 105th Congress, Republican efforts to rewrite the nation's medical malpractice laws did not succeed. The issue, however, is expected to resurface during the 106th Congress. Attempts may be made to

- Limit noneconomic damages in malpractice litigation;
- Require periodic payments for large settlements;
- Impose limitations on contingent fee arrangements under which attorneys receive a percentage of any money collected by the plaintiff as a result of a suit;
- Institute alternative dispute mechanisms, such as mediation or arbitration; and
- Require the losing party to pay attorneys' fees.

Noneconomic damages are compensation for losses, such as physical and emotional pain, suffering, inconvenience, physical impairment, mental anguish, disfigurement, and loss of enjoyment of life. These damages differ from economic losses, which are easily measured and consist of hospital and medical expenses, lost wages, and lost employment. Although the valuation of noneconomic damages is more subjective, they are nevertheless real losses that may result from malpractice.

Many states already have enacted medical liability reform. They differ, however, in their treatment of noneconomic losses. California and several other states have adopted a cap or statutory limit on the amount of noneconomic damages a plaintiff may receive. Other states, as well as the federal government, impose no limits. Federal malpractice reform would impose a uniform standard on all states. In 1998, as part of the Republican plan to provide more consumer protections under managed care, the House of Representatives passed a malpractice provision to limit noneconomic damages to $250,000. That bill was not considered on the floor of the Senate.

ANA POSITION

ANA opposes arbitrary caps on noneconomic damages that limit victims' access to compensation. In the absence of meaningful quality controls on health care, access to the judicial system is an important means of ensuring accountability, especially from health care institutions.

Managed Care

ISSUE

Changes in the health care delivery system under managed care.

BACKGROUND

The concept of managed care has evolved in recent years from specific types of delivery systems to current arrangements that often include elements from several systems. Providers have had to tailor their practices to accommodate the demands of this market-driven form of health care delivery.

Managed care plans traditionally have been more generous with preventive services than fee-for-service plans. Some plans create financial incentives for providers to contain costs by paying them a fixed amount per enrollee per month for a defined bundle of services. In some instances, enrollees are required to have a referral from a primary care gatekeeper before receiving care from a specialist. In an effort to encourage treatment in less costly settings and with less costly interventions, plans may require preauthorization of hospital admissions and may require practitioners to justify treatment decisions that exceed the norms of established guidelines. As these practices have become more common, consumers and providers have become increasingly concerned that the quality of health care services is suffering because of an inappropriate concentration on cost containment.

ANA POSITION

Managed care presents opportunities as well as risks for nurses and their patients. The search for cost-effective, high-quality care creates openings for nurses to serve as case managers, care coordinators, and alternatives to more costly sources of care. The risk of arbitrary or unfair exclusion from network plans, however, may threaten these opportunities. Moreover, managed care has had a major impact on hospital use. The consequent reduction in hospital staffing has included nurses at these facilities. In managed care organizations, maintaining patients' access to services and the quality of care presents both risks and opportunities for the nursing profession.

ANA has adopted managed care principles that emphasize the right of individuals to

- Access health care services along the full continuum of care;
- Empower consumers as partners in making health care decisions;
- Recognize the need for interdisciplinary collaboration among providers;
- Support value-based health care services to maximize quality and control costs;
- Provide appropriate attention to the health of individuals, families, communities, and populations;
- Promote the provision of cultural and linguistic competence in the delivery of services;
- Support high standards of ethical behavior;
- Share accountability among health systems, plans, providers, and consumers;
- Protect the confidentiality of patient information; and
- Ensure the right to a safe and healthy work environment for all health care providers.

Medicaid

ISSUE

Continued federal support for quality health care services for Medicaid beneficiaries; continuing and expanding coverage of advanced practice nurse (APN) services.

BACKGROUND

The Medicaid program is a joint federal-state medical assistance program that was initiated in 1965 with the goal of providing health care coverage to low-income individuals.

Medicaid is financed by both federal and state funds. The federal government pays about 55 percent of Medicaid's costs. Each state designs and administers its own program under the general oversight of the Health Care Financing Administration (HCFA), which is charged with ensuring compliance with federal standards and requirements. In fiscal year 1997, the cost of federal Medicaid grants to the states totaled $103 billion.

Among the reimbursable services that states are required to include in their Medicaid programs are those of certified nurse midwives (CNMs), certified family nurse practitioners (FNPs), and certified pediatric nurse practitioners (PNPs).

The Balanced Budget Act of 1997 created a system for states to use for Medicaid-managed care, using a primary care case manager or gatekeeper approach. This model follows the approach that previously had been adopted in many states through HCFA waivers of the fee-for-service model that had been the basis for Medicaid reimbursement. The new law allows states to determine whether or not APNs may be primary care case managers. In states in which physicians only are permitted to serve as case managers, APN services are not available to many consumers.

ANA POSITION

ANA supports expansion of the Medicaid program to increase access to underserved populations. ANA opposes attempts to cut off Medicaid recipients' access to APN services and will work to bring the primary care case management role in line with the current federal mandate to cover CNM, FNP, and PNP services.

Medicare

ISSUE

Adequate funding of the Medicare program to ensure availability of quality, accessible services for Medicare beneficiaries.

BACKGROUND

The Medicare program was established in 1965 with the goal of providing quality health care to the nation's elderly and disabled. Today the program faces a growing financial crisis as health care costs increase and the Medicare-eligible population continues to grow.

Medicare consists of two main parts. Part A, also known as the Hospital Insurance Trust Fund, pays the cost of hospital inpatient and skilled nursing care. Anyone age 65 or older who is eligible for Social Security or for railroad retirement benefits automatically is eligible for Part A benefits. Other eligible individuals include people under 65 years of age who receive Social Security disability benefits or railroad retirement disability, and people with end-stage kidney disease. People age 65 or older not otherwise eligible can buy coverage. Part A is financed primarily by a 1.45 percent payroll tax collected through Social Security withholding. Because of increases in health care costs and the growing number of beneficiaries, the trust fund is projected to go bankrupt in fiscal year 2008 unless changes are made. The trust fund's viability was extended from fiscal year 2001 to 2008 due to changes made in the Balanced Budget Act of 1997 (Public Law 105-33).

Medicare Part B, also known as the Supplemental Medical Insurance program, is an optional add-on taken by almost all individuals covered by Part A. Part B pays 80 percent of covered doctor and outpatient charges after an annual $100 deductible. Monthly premiums finance about 25 percent of the costs of Part B. Most of the balance is financed by general taxpayer revenues.

The Bipartisan Commission on the Future of Medicare, which was created by the Balanced Budget Act of 1997, was unable to reach consensus on a Medicare Reform plan by the March 1999 deadline established in the public law. Consequently, several members of Congress and the administration are developing Medicare reform proposals that will be debated in the 106th Congress.

ANA POSITION

ANA released its Medicare reform proposal in March 1999. That proposal reaffirms ANA's long-standing commitment to strengthen the Medicare program; recommends that much of its structure remain the same; and includes recommendations to simplify and improve the program to better meet the diverse health care needs of a growing population of older Americans. In addition to structural improvements, ANA's proposal includes recommendations about how to raise the additional revenues needed to address the Medicare program's projected shortfall and the additional costs incurred by adopting the enhancements proposed by ANA.

...ment and End-of-Life Care

...s to effective pain and symptom management and palliative care for chronic-pain ...tients and those who are terminally ill.

...CKGROUND

In the United States pain often is left untreated or under-treated, even though 50 percent of patients experience moderate to severe pain at least half the time in their last days of life and pain often is cited as a reason individuals seek physician-assisted suicide.

Assisted suicide, which now is permitted by law in some circumstances in Oregon, is the subject of tremendous controversy throughout the United States. This controversy and the Oregon law have led to different legislative approaches at the national level. Because of the Oregon law, legislation intended to prevent physician-assisted suicide by making controlled drugs unavailable for this purpose was considered in the 105th Congress. Patient advocacy and provider organizations, including those such as ANA that have actively opposed assisted suicide, opposed this legislation because of the chilling effect it would have had on appropriate pain management. The bill would have provided for investigations by the Drug Enforcement Administration (DEA) using as the standard the private intentions of the health care professionals involved in the prescription of medication. Opponents believed this provision would be intimidating and counterproductive. Furthermore, the bill would have done nothing to address assisted suicide by means other than controlled substances.

Another approach, developed by a coalition of advocacy and provider organizations, would enact a new federal law to coordinate efforts to improve access to high-quality, effective pain and symptom management and palliative care to ensure that the needs of chronic-pain and terminally ill patients are met. Although such an initiative is not intended solely as a response to the assisted-suicide debate, advocates believe that successful interventions of this type obviate the demand for the assisted-suicide option.

ANA POSITION

ANA has been active in efforts to prohibit assisted suicide. It is strongly committed to the principle that the role of medical and nursing professionals is to heal and relieve those in pain, not act to end a life or to make the means of death available to people seeking to end their life. ANA also opposes legislation that would have a chilling effect on pain management and result in needless suffering, which is a result totally at odds with the professional commitment of the nursing profession. Nurses have long been in the forefront as leaders and advocates for the delivery of dignified and human end-of-life care and are obligated to provide relief of suffering and comfort to a dying person. The legal system must not create barriers to appropriate palliative care, which is an ethical mandate for the profession.

Patient Privacy and Confidentiality

ISSUE

Patient's right to privacy, protection of information, and access to records.

BACKGROUND

Advances in technology have facilitated the collection and dissemination of important health care data, both in the aggregate and the tracking of individual patient records. This ability is important for both research efforts and individual patients in our increasingly mobile society and changing health care system in which patients frequently are seen by a variety of health care providers in a variety of settings. The Health Insurance Portability and Accountability Act of 1996 (HIPAA) (Public Law 104-191) sets out new requirements for administrative simplification that ANA believes could help streamline administrative processes, reduce duplication of administrative data collection, and provide consistency and reliability in the transmission and comparison of data.

These advances, however, also have made it more difficult to ensure that a patient's basic right to privacy is protected. There is not a federal standard that governs access to and control over health records. Patients have a statutory right to examine their own records in only 28 states. HIPAA, however, stipulates that if Congress has not passed comprehensive health privacy legislation by August 21, 1999, the Secretary of Health and Human Services must issue regulations by February 2000.

In addition to basic concerns about the right to privacy, inappropriate disclosure of information can lead to discrimination in employment or insurance. Legislation also may be proposed to safeguard individuals from adverse insurance and employment treatment on the basis of genetic information or a history of domestic violence.

ANA POSITION

ANA believes that any statutory changes with respect to patient privacy should be approached with caution. Changes must ensure that nurses are not compromised in their ability to adhere to the standards in the Code for Nurses. The Code requires that nurses safeguard the patient's right to privacy by protecting information of a confidential nature, and that the rights, well-being, and safety of the patient should be the determining factors when arriving at any professional judgment concerning the disposition of confidential information. Information documenting the appropriateness, necessity, and quality of care required for the purposes of peer review, third-party payment, and other quality-assurance mechanisms must be disclosed only under defined policies, mandates, or protocols. Individuals should maintain right-of-control over information in their records. ANA supports legislation to protect individuals from adverse consequences based on genetic information or a history of domestic violence.

Telehealth

ISSUE

Maximization of the appropriate use of telecommunications technology in the delivery of health care.

BACKGROUND

Advances in telecommunications technology have provided opportunities for the delivery of health care in ways that would have been impossible a few years ago. These advances allow health care providers to transmit and receive information when the patient is far away.

Although these advances offer many opportunities to provide health care to patients who currently do not have access to health care providers (generally because they live in rural areas where there is a shortage of health care providers), it also presents challenges when determining the appropriate standards of care. The possibility exists that telecommunications technologies may be used to control health care costs by keeping patients who could see a health care provider from doing so.

ANA successfully lobbied for a provision in the Balanced Budget Act of 1997 (Public Law 105-33) that provides for Medicare reimbursement for telehealth services in certain underserved rural areas. ANA now is working with the Health Care Financing Administration (HCFA) to ensure appropriate implementation of that law.

In the 105th Congress, legislation was introduced to provide grants and loans to establish telehealth networks in rural and underserved areas. This legislation is very sensitive to nursing concerns and broadens the scope of federal government involvement beyond "telemedicine" to the full spectrum of "telehealth." It also is careful to focus telehealth services on areas that are underserved so that telehealth will not become a substitute for traditional health care in areas where face-to-face provider visits already are available.

ANA POSITION

ANA supports federal efforts to use telehealth to bring health care to those who do not have adequate access to health care. ANA does not support the use of telehealth in lieu of a visit with a licensed health care provider in order to control costs or reduce access to health care. ANA supports efforts that appropriately use telehealth to help patients receive care from a licensed health care provider in areas where access to health care providers is inadequate.

2

ANA/SNA Organizational Viability

Campaign Finance Reform

ISSUE

Reform of campaign finance laws to limit spending on congressional campaigns.

BACKGROUND

Concerns over the financing of congressional elections have focused on the high cost of campaigns and the prominent role of political action committees (PACs) as a source of funding. Spending by 1996 House and Senate general election candidates exceeded $626 million, up 60 percent since 1990. Increasingly expensive elections have fostered the view that spending is out of control, too much time is spent raising funds, and elections are "bought and sold."

The increasing cost of getting elected is generating a growing reliance on PAC contributions. The importance of PAC contributions in relation to other funding sources is revealed in data that show 29 percent of House and Senate candidates' receipts came from PACs in 1996. This figure was up from 15.7 percent in 1974, but down from a high of 33.7 percent in 1988.

Congress signaled its willingness to consider changes in the campaign finance laws in August 1986 (99th Congress) when the Senate passed the Boren-Goldwater Amendment, which featured an aggregate limit on the receipt of PAC contributions by House and Senate candidates and a lower PAC contribution limit. Although no vote was taken on the legislation to which the Boren-Goldwater Amendment was attached (thereby "killing" the initiative), passage of the amendment itself marked the first time since 1979 that either body of Congress had voted to impose new regulations on the flow of money in federal elections. Legislative activity intensified in the 100th, 101st, 102nd, 103rd, and 104th Congresses, although no legislation was ever enacted into law. In August 1998 campaign finance reform passed the House. That measure would have banned so-called "soft money" contributions to the political parties and curbed unregulated "issue-advocacy" advertising that refers to candidates in a pre-election period. Campaign finance reform died in the 105th Congress, after it was blocked by a Senate filibuster. The sponsors of the House-passed bill are planning to renew their efforts in the 106th Congress.

ANA POSITION

ANA believes that excessive spending on congressional campaigns deters women and minority candidates from running for Congress. However, ANA opposes the elimination of PACs. ANA believes that PACs are instrumental in involving ordinary citizens in the electoral process and considers ANA-PAC critical to the involvement of individual nurses in that process. During the 1997–1998 election cycle, ANA-PAC's integrated mail/phone fundraising campaign raised more than $1 million. More than 20,000 individual nurses contributed to ANA-PAC in that two-year period. The average contribution was $45. ANA-PAC endorsed 252 candidates for the U.S. Senate and House of Representatives in the 1998 general election. Of those candidates, 88 percent, including three nurses, won their elections and are members of the 106th Congress.

Employee Retirement Income Security Act Reform

ISSUE

Adequate regulation of health care plans that fall outside the purview of state insurance regulations.

BACKGROUND

The Employee Retirement Income Security Act (ERISA), which was passed in 1974, places the regulation of pensions and other employee benefit plans, including health plans, under federal jurisdiction. Although ERISA contains extensive regulations related to pensions, it contains few regulatory requirements for health plans. The Department of Labor (DOL) is primarily responsible for enforcing this statute. Under ERISA states have the authority to regulate health insurance plans sold to employers by commercial carriers. ERISA, however, also preempts or excludes from state regulation health plans provided by employers who self-insure. In some areas, more than half of the population receives health care coverage through employers who self-insure and thus do not receive protections, such as benefit and disclosure requirements generally required by state insurance regulations. Furthermore, because malpractice statutes are not part of the "business of insurance" that is left to state regulation, health insurance plans cannot be sued in state courts for harmful denials of health care coverage. ERISA itself allows for such minimal recovery that it is not worth bringing such suits in federal court.

The Health Insurance Portability and Accountability Act (Public Law 104-191), which was enacted in 1996, was drafted so that its protections apply to all types of health insurance, including ERISA plans. This action, though limited in scope, has provided an avenue for better insurance protections for persons covered by ERISA plans. Numerous bills were introduced in the 105th Congress, including comprehensive patient protection reforms, using this framework. Only one bill, which required plans to cover reconstructive surgery for mastectomy patients, was actually enacted.

There have been efforts in recent years to exempt Multiple Employer Welfare Arrangements (MEWAs) from state regulation and place them instead under ERISA. Proponents of this deregulation are renewing their efforts in the 106th Congress. MEWAs, which allow small employers to band together to purchase employee benefit coverage including health insurance, have a history of fraud and undercapitalization. Given the weakness inherent in the health plan protections in ERISA law, there is considerable concern that moving more plans into the current ERISA structure would mean a significant loss of consumer health care protections.

ANA POSITION

ANA favors stronger regulation of self-insured health plans and will oppose efforts to increase the scope of ERISA coverage, such as exempting MEWAs from state regulation. ANA strongly supports efforts to extend basic consumer protections to enrollees of all health plans, including redress for damages so that accountability is shared among health plans, health systems, providers, and consumers.

Permanent Replacement of Striking Workers

ISSUE

Protection of legally striking workers against discrimination and permanent replacement.

BACKGROUND

Although employers have had the legal authority to hire permanent replacements for striking employees since 1938, this practice did not become popular until President Reagan fired striking air traffic controllers in 1981 and hired permanent replacements. A General Accounting Office (GAO) report shows that employers announced their intention to hire permanent striker replacements in about one in four of the strikes reported between 1985 and 1989. Both management and union officials report that the current practice of hiring permanent replacements occurs more frequently than it did in the late 1970s.

Nurses across the country have used the right to strike as a last-resort effort to improve patient care and working conditions, and to retain health benefits for themselves and their families. Following a strike involving registered nurses (RNs) in Minnesota, a reporter for the *Philadelphia Inquirer* wrote: "The nurses were successful in telling the public that they are a quality-care profession. This was really a strike that benefited the entire nation."

Nurses who have participated in strikes have faced retaliation. Some have lost permanent shifts won through seniority, been denied opportunities to participate in continuing education programs, or been given only the most difficult assignments and heaviest patient loads. Some nurses have lost full-time jobs and been given only part-time work. Others have been replaced permanently.

The United States is the only industrialized nation that permits the permanent replacement of workers who strike. Japan, France, and West Germany, the United States' key economic competitors, all categorically reject the idea of dismissing striking workers.

If employers are permitted to permanently replace striking nurses, or to discriminate against them for participating in a strike, nurses have little power at the bargaining table.

ANA POSITION

ANA believes it is critical that the balance of power in employer-nurses labor relations should not be skewed by the threat of loss of employment held over nurses' heads. ANA supports legislation that bars permanent replacement of striking workers and prohibits discrimination against those who participate in strikes. ANA believes that federal policy should protect the rights of workers.

3

_Care for
Underserved
and Special
Populations_

Domestic Violence

ISSUE

Elimination of all forms of domestic violence.

BACKGROUND

Violence within families is responsible for numerous injuries. Although the solution to the problem requires a total community effort, nurses and other health care providers can play a special role. Health care providers must be responsive to the emotional and physical well-being of victims of domestic violence and must aid in the prevention of further violence and abuse.

The Violence Against Women Act (VAWA) became law in the 103rd Congress. It provided funding for programs and grants to develop and strengthen effective law enforcement and prosecution strategies to combat violent crimes against women. Although the 105th Congress was unable to enact the Violence Against Women Act II (VAWAII), some of its provisions passed as riders on other legislation. The Higher Education Reauthorization Act included a $10 million grant program for campuses to fight rape and sexual assault.

A revised VAWAII will be introduced in the 106th Congress. It will address the impact of violence on children; the needs of older, disabled, and immigrant women who are battered; and safety in the workplace. VAWAII will prohibit employers from taking adverse job actions against employees who are victims of violent crimes and will provide for training for local law enforcement, judicial staff, and health professionals working with victims of domestic violence, rape, and sexual assault. VAWAII will also include provisions to stop all types of insurance companies from discriminating against victims of domestic violence.

ANA POSITION

ANA is committed to taking a leadership role in addressing domestic abuse through legislative, regulatory, and health care arenas. ANA is particularly concerned about the impact of child abuse and other forms of domestic violence on children.

Specifically, ANA supports

- Establishment of a national data collection center for domestic abuse statistics;
- Requirements for mandatory reporting of domestic abuse at the national and state levels by health care professionals;
- Increased federal funding for emergency and transitional shelters;
- Funding for advocacy services for domestic abuse victims; and
- Educational programs for nurses, physicians, and other health care workers on domestic abuse awareness and prevention.

ANA believes that crisis intervention programs and shelters for victims of domestic violence must be accessible in both rural and metropolitan areas.

HIV/AIDS

ISSUE

Federal support of research, prevention, and care programs to combat the human immunodeficiency virus (HIV) and federal infection control policies that ensure public health and maintain worker protection.

BACKGROUND

HIV has been declared a major health priority for the United States and the world. New estimates from the Joint United Nations Programme on HIV/acquired immune deficiency syndrome (AIDS) (UNAIDS) and the World Health Organization (WHO) show that by the end of 1998 the number of people living with HIV (the virus that causes AIDS) had grown to 33.4 million. This is an increase of more than 10 percent from 1997. According to new UNAIDS/WHO estimates, 11 men, women, and children around the world were infected each minute in 1998, close to 6 million people in all. One-tenth of newly infected people were under age 15, which brings the number of children with HIV to 1.2 million.

Centers for Disease Control and Prevention (CDC) statistics confirm that the proportion of AIDS cases among women, racial/ethnic minorities, and children will continue to increase. Since the start of the epidemic approximately two decades ago, HIV has infected more than 47 million people and taken the lives of nearly 14 million adults and children. In 1998 alone, nearly 75,000 people became infected with HIV.

AIDS continues to stress an already overburdened urban public health care system and is now further eroding a rural health care system that traditionally has demonstrated difficulty providing access to health care for all.

The use of early drug treatments for HIV-positive but asymptomatic persons has increased the need for early identification and counseling and increased the cost of care. Access to early treatments for vulnerable high-risk persons has increased the need for Medicaid expansion and community-based care.

President Clinton has voiced a strong commitment to fighting the AIDS epidemic. In the 105th Congress, legislation was enacted as part of the fiscal year 1999 appropriations process that provided $156 million in additional funding for minority communities to help ensure access to antiretroviral drug therapy for those already living with HIV.

ANA POSITION

ANA supports increased funding for research, education, and prevention services to prevent the spread of HIV and opposes any restrictions on educational or prevention programs. ANA advocates increased funding for drug rehabilitation programs, early intervention, and outreach programs. ANA is opposed to discrimination against persons with HIV in the provision of health care, employment, housing, and insurance. ANA opposes policies that impose travel or immigration restrictions on those with HIV/AIDS. ANA is opposed to mandatory HIV testing of patients and health care professionals, but supports voluntary, anonymous HIV testing with informed consent, confidentiality, and pre- and post-test counseling.

Long-Term Care

ISSUE

Access to comprehensive, coordinated, and cost-effective long-term care for all individuals who require it, as well as protection of individuals from the catastrophic costs of long-term care.

BACKGROUND

Most long-term care services are needed in homes, rather than institutions, although up to 80 percent of all Americans will need institutional long-term care services sometime in their lives. Nearly one-third of those who need long-term care are under the age of 65. Currently, most long-term care services are paid through out-of-pocket expenses or Medicaid, the federal/state program for low-income individuals and families. Less than 10 percent of Americans have private long-term care insurance or coverage under Medicaid. The need for long-term care services is expected to grow as the size of the elderly population doubles over the next 40 years. The cost of such care generally is prohibitive. The only option for most Americans is to "spend down" to become eligible for Medicaid. Many elderly individuals must impoverish themselves to receive needed health care services.

Medicare benefits currently provide only brief institutional long-term care services and limited home-health nursing services for noninstitutionalized persons who live in the community. These persons would benefit from increased access to and coverage by Medicare of programs such as adult day care, alternative living arrangements, family/friend care giving and other informal support, medical transportation, homemaker services, and personal and respite care. These programs and a wide array of other services may be necessary to enable disabled and frail elderly individuals to avoid institutionalization.

Designing a long-term system is difficult because society as a whole has not determined the goals of long-term care.

ANA POSITION

ANA supports community-based health care delivery, nursing care, and nurse-coordinated case management. ANA actively monitors and supports measures to refine quality improvement mechanisms currently in place for long-term care. ANA supports reform of long-term care insurance to incorporate appropriate insurance standards. ANA is working with coalitions of health care-related organizations and federal commissions to advance these proposals.

Mental Health

ISSUE

Increased access to adequate and appropriate mental health treatment.

BACKGROUND

Mental illness and addictive disorders cause personal, economic, and social upheaval for individuals and families. Between 30 and 45 million Americans suffer from diagnosable mental disorders involving disabilities in employment, attendance at school, or independent living. Direct and indirect expenses, including long-term care, Social Security disability, lost productivity, and health care expenditures exceed $185 billion annually.

Legislation enacted in 1996 requires group health insurance plans that cover mental illness to set the same annual and lifetime coverage limits for both mental illness and physical illness. The requirement does not apply to companies with 50 or fewer employees and will be waived for larger companies if it causes their premiums to rise 1 percent or more. This limited step toward mental health parity was a compromise forged after the Senate passed a proposal that would have required health insurance plans to provide equal coverage in all respects for mental and physical ailments.

ANA POSITION

ANA supports coverage of inpatient and outpatient mental health services as a standard benefit. ANA supports parity for mental health and physical illness services as well as efforts that address mental health outcome research and service evaluation.

Native American Health Care

ISSUE

Funding for health care programs authorized under the Indian Health Care Improvement Act.

BACKGROUND

The federal government is mandated by treaties and legislation to provide health care to Native Americans (including native Alaskans and Hawaiians) to ensure that the health status of the American Indian is equivalent to that of the rest of the nation.

Despite the provision of services through the Indian Health Service (IHS) programs, Native Americans' health status is still several decades behind the rest of the population. Although infant mortality has decreased in recent years, the incidences of tuberculosis and drug and alcohol abuse exceed the rates for other underserved and minority Americans.

IHS was reauthorized by the Indian Health Amendments of 1992. The reauthorizing legislation supports a comprehensive health care program that includes a direct health care delivery system, a tribal health care delivery system using contracts with tribes and tribal groups, and the purchase of contract care from nontribal providers. Health education and prevention activities are provided by community health and public health nurses. Included in the reauthorizing legislation was the expansion of nursing services through the utilization of clinics run by nursing schools.

Nursing represents approximately two-thirds of the professional staff that provides direct patient care through the IHS. The chief nurse (renamed nurse consultant) is responsible for providing leadership and direction for the nursing service. Despite special pay rates, IHS still experiences a severe shortage of nurses. Fortunately, the trend has been to increase appropriations for incentive programs to assist in the recruitment and retention of nurses in the IHS. The Indian Health Care Improvement Act is due for reauthorization in fiscal year 2000. ANA will work to ensure that nursing education programs within the IHS are maintained during the reauthorization process.

ANA POSITION

ANA supports the maintenance of and increased funding for the programs represented in the Indian Health Care Improvement Act of 1992, including programs for alcohol and drug abuse. ANA believes that improved access to health care and the improved health status of Native Americans can be facilitated by recruitment and retention efforts directed at increasing the number of Native Americans who provide health care. These efforts include increased special pay, health scholarships for Native Americans, and targeted loans for nurses and other health care workers who provide care to Native Americans. ANA also is concerned about the role of nurses in the IHS. ANA supports efforts to restore the chief nurse position in the director's office to further integrate and coordinate nursing and health care services.

Rural Health Care

ISSUE

Federal programs to address the unmet health care needs of rural residents.

BACKGROUND

The nation's rural health care system is unable to provide accessible, high-quality health care services to rural consumers. Frequently, there is a shortage in the number, type, and distribution of qualified health care providers in rural communities. Compared with urban residents, rural Americans have a higher infant mortality rate and a higher incidence of occupational injuries. There also is a greater prevalence of serious health conditions in rural America. Disease prevention, health promotion, and case management programs are hampered by economic barriers, such as inadequate or unavailable health insurance coverage, and by factors such as transportation.

In rural areas there is a shortage of registered nurses (RNs), including advanced practice nurses (APNs). Only 18 percent of all RNs are available to serve the 25 percent of the population that lives in rural areas. One reason for this disparity is that rural nurses receive lower salaries and benefits than their urban counterparts. Other reasons may include professional isolation, a lack of continuing education opportunities, and an inability to be reimbursed directly for providing primary health care services characteristic of rural versus urban nurses.

Rural nursing has received increased attention, as evidenced by the increase in undergraduate and graduate nursing programs with a rural health care focus. The Health Professions Education Extension Amendments of 1992 targeted nursing education in rural areas by giving preference to schools with a track record of graduates who practice in rural areas.

ANA POSITION

ANA believes that rural residents have a right to accessible, high-quality, comprehensive, and coordinated health care services. Although recent federal initiatives have addressed the rural nursing shortage, issues such as the disparity between urban and rural nurse compensation and wage compression still must be resolved. ANA supports tax incentives, rural hospital differentials, and nurse workforce initiatives to help address these problems.

4

Nursing Economics

(Compensation and Reimbursement)

Collective Bargaining

ISSUE

Preservation of nurses' rights to engage in collective bargaining.

BACKGROUND

Nurses have been involved in collective bargaining since 1946. State nurses associations (SNAs) represent more registered nurses (RNs) for collective bargaining purposes than any other union. SNAs are recognized at the bargaining table as leaders in securing strong contracts for the nurses they represent.

Along with the traditional wage and benefits concerns, SNA-negotiated contracts address such issues as nursing roles, nonnursing duties, appropriate staffing, practice-related committees, professional standards, staff development, and occupational health and safety. Nurses have bargained successfully for across-the-board pay hikes, bonus systems, rewards for experience and length of service, increases in differential pay, language recognizing that delegation of tasks is not supervisory work, and protection from replacement by unlicensed technicians.

In today's rapidly changing health care environment, collective bargaining has proven to be one of the most effective ways to protect patients from inadequate and unsafe care and to ensure that nurses have fair pay, good benefits, and satisfactory working conditions. For many nurses, collective bargaining has been the means through which they have achieved professional autonomy.

ANA POSITION

Legislative and regulatory efforts continue to try to dismantle current labor protections and generate opposition to measures that would improve workplace protection and workers' rights and benefits. A weak labor movement and policy interpretations that support business have encouraged employers to invest in costly, aggressive efforts to avoid unionization and made it more difficult to organize and represent workers.

ANA believes that nurses have a professional responsibility and an ethical duty to maintain employment conditions conducive to high-quality nursing care. Collective bargaining provides a legitimate mechanism for nurses to resolve conflicts that prevent the delivery of high-quality nursing care and to improve wages, benefits, and working conditions.

ANA supports legislative initiatives that protect the rights of workers and improve opportunities for collective bargaining.

Entry of Foreign-Educated Nurses

ISSUE

Employment of foreign-educated nurses through temporary visas.

BACKGROUND

In September 1995, the H-1A temporary visa program used by the majority of foreign-educated nurses to enter the United States expired. Foreign-educated nurses now can enter the United States via several other vehicles:

- The H-1B visa is a temporary visa program for all professionals.
- The H-2B visa is a temporary visa used for periods of entry less than one year.
- The employment-based visa allows permanent entry.
- The North American Free Trade Agreement (NAFTA) has provisions that allow Canadian and Mexican nurses to enter the United States.

With passage of the Illegal Immigration Reform and Immigrant Responsibility Act of 1996, all foreign health care professionals, except physicians, must be certified by the Commission on Graduates of Foreign Nursing Schools (CGFNS) or another independent, government-certified organization qualified to issue credentials. The certification process must verify that the foreign health care worker's education, training, or experience meets all applicable statutory and regulatory requirements for entry into the United States. In addition, any foreign license submitted by the foreign health care worker must be validated as authentic and unencumbered. If the health care worker is a registered nurse (RN), the nurse must have passed an examination testing both nursing skill and English language proficiency. ANA strongly supported this legislation.

Also passed in 1996 was a measure that extended, until September 30, 1997, the visa period for nurses already in the United States on existing H-1A visas.

ANA POSITION

ANA believes that the root causes for the instability of the nursing workforce, which has led to swings in the supply and demand of nurses, must be addressed. Overreliance on foreign-educated nurses by the hospital industry serves only to postpone efforts required to address the needs of the U.S. nursing workforce. ANA considers the extension of the H-1A visa to September 30, 1997, to be a phase-in period during which H-1A nurses must either obtain permanent citizenship or make plans to return to their home country. ANA does not support any further extension or restoration of the H-1A visa program.

ANA considers the certification process to apply to all foreign-educated health care workers regardless of whether they enter the United States via a temporary entry visa, permanent employment-based visa, or NAFTA. ANA opposes efforts to exempt foreign-educated nurses from the current H-1B requirements.

ANA supports strengthening the labor requirements for U.S. employers that seek to bring in workers under employment-based visas.

Fair Labor Standards Act

ISSUE

Use of compensatory time off in lieu of overtime pay.

BACKGROUND

The Fair Labor Standards Act (FLSA) was enacted in 1938 in reaction to the economic and social problems that existed during the Great Depression. Congress sought to establish minimum work standards to encourage employment. FLSA sets the standard for minimum wages, overtime compensation, equal pay, 40-hour work week, and child labor for all employees covered by the act. In regard to overtime pay, FLSA requires employers to pay overtime at a rate one-and-one-half times the employee's regular rate of pay for all hours worked over 40 per week.

Current proposals under consideration by Congress would amend FLSA to allow private sector employers to compensate their employees for overtime with compensatory time off, instead of the overtime pay required by current law. Employers would "pay" one-and-one-half hours of compensatory time for each hour worked over 40 in a work week. Employees could accrue up to 30 days of compensatory time per year. Although employers would be prohibited from making a compensatory time agreement a condition of employment, they would be able to refuse the time off if the compensatory time places an "undue burden" on the business.

ANA POSITION

ANA supports flexible hours when employees have sufficient control over their participation in the program and use of their compensatory time. Without these stringent protections, ANA believes that such proposals undermine the standard 40-hour work week established by FLSA.

Although current proposals would make taking time off in lieu of overtime pay voluntary, ANA is concerned that such practices might become the accepted norm and that noncompliance could lead to the employee being ostracized or, more significantly, retaliated against by the employer.

Global Trade Agreements

ISSUE

Impact of global trade agreements on nurses.

BACKGROUND

The North American Free Trade Agreement (NAFTA) is a multilateral pact between the United States, Mexico, and Canada that loosens restrictions on trade among the three countries. The nursing profession had great concerns about the sections in NAFTA that relate to the provision of cross-border professional services. ANA received written clarification from the Office of the U.S. Trade Representative that NAFTA does not eliminate any government authority to regulate professional services or establish regulations in the future. The procedures currently in use in the United States to test, evaluate, and certify professional competency continue under NAFTA. NAFTA encourages, but does not require, all three countries to work toward recognizing each other's licenses and certifications.

The Uruguay Round Agreements under the General Agreement on Tariffs and Trades (GATT) was passed by the 103rd Congress. This agreement, for the first time, provides for the establishment of a multilateral framework that covers services, including health care services. The agreement includes language that maintains the primacy of state laws, including licensure laws.

With the passage of these agreements, the United States has entered into an era of expanding trade, including services, with far fewer restrictions and barriers.

ANA POSITION

ANA believes that the current system of accreditation, licensure, and professional education, coupled with high professional standards in nursing, is essential to protect U.S. consumers from unsafe and inadequate health care. ANA will work to ensure that consumers receive quality care from licensed professionals who have met exacting standards.

ANA believes that the nursing community must investigate which model(s) of international mobility will best serve the interests of our patients, our health care systems, and professional nursing in the United States.

ANA is extremely concerned about the ability of the Immigration and Naturalization Service (INS) and related agencies to adequately track and monitor the number of professionals entering the United States under NAFTA. As a result of poor data collection and follow up, it is extremely difficult to determine the impact trade agreements are having on the domestic workforce. ANA believes that before further trade agreements are negotiated and approved, a better system of data collection and monitoring must be put into place.

Social Security

ISSUE

Adequate funding for the Social Security program.

BACKGROUND

The Social Security program was established in 1935 to provide income to retirees. In addition to retirement benefits, Social Security provides benefits for workers who become disabled. The full-retirement age currently is 65, although an individual may retire as early as age 62 with reduced benefits.

Social Security is financed primarily through payroll taxes. This income goes directly to meet current benefit obligations. The program is not, as is popularly believed, financed by individual accounts that a worker pays into when working and then draws from when retired.

Given the future growth of the elderly population once the "baby boom" generation starts retiring, Social Security is facing a long-term funding crisis. Because the program counts on the income of current workers to fund the benefits of current retirees, the demographic shift will have serious negative consequences for the Social Security Trust Fund.

There are a number of proposals that address this issue. One proposal would allow individuals to invest some of the money they would pay in Social Security taxes in the stock market or other investment vehicles. Another proposal suggests the government invest a portion of the money it collects for Social Security in the stock market. Other proposals would set aside a portion of the anticipated federal budget surplus to be used for Social Security.

One issue raised by supporters of the current system is that Social Security provides a public "safety net" by increasing the payments lower-income beneficiaries receive. Many of the proposals that would allow individuals to invest Social Security money themselves lose that element of social insurance.

ANA POSITION

ANA believes Social Security needs to be maintained as a strong, viable program that will meet the needs of those who count on its benefits. ANA supports maintaining the social insurance component of the current Social Security program and believes policy-makers need to address the long-term financing needs of the program to ensure that it remains viable. Because more than 70 percent of the population over age 85 are women and women typically have a greater need for Social Security, nursing needs to work toward maintaining the viability of this program.

Third-Party Reimbursement

ISSUE

Federal policies that call for equitable reimbursement for services delivered by all advanced practice nurses (APNs), including nurse practitioners (NPs), clinical nurse specialists (CNSs), certified nurse midwives (CNMs), and certified registered nurse anesthetists (CRNAs).

BACKGROUND

As a result of the Balanced Budget Act of 1997 (Public Law 105-33), the services of NPs and CNSs now are eligible for Medicare Part B coverage and direct reimbursement regardless of the geographic area in which they are provided. This provision is the result of almost eight years of work by ANA to provide Medicare beneficiaries access to the services of NPs and CNSs.

The law defines covered physician services to include services provided by an NP or a CNS when those services would be considered physician's services if provided by a physician. Basically, this means that if the service would be covered under Medicare Part B when provided by a physician, it can be covered when provided by an NP or a CNS.

The Medicare fee schedule sets payments at 85 percent of the fee a physician would be paid for the same service. The new law contains language excluding payment for some services if a facility or provider charges or is paid any amount for those services.

The law currently requires state Medicaid programs to provide direct reimbursement to certified pediatric nurse practitioners (PNPs), certified family nurse practitioners (FNPs), and CNMs. Some states have opted to cover the services of other APNs. Other states have chosen not to include APN services beyond the federal mandate. Although states set their own reimbursement rates for Medicaid providers, payment levels must be adequate to ensure that Medicaid beneficiaries have access to covered services comparable to those available to the general population.

ANA POSITION

Every American must have access to and coverage for high-quality preventive, primary, acute, and community-care services. As cost-effective sources of quality care, APNs can enhance patients' access to vital care, particularly in underserved rural and urban areas. APNs make health care affordable, available, acceptable, and accountable.

Direct Medicaid reimbursement should be provided to all APNs, without regard for the geographic location, practice setting, or category of APN. In addition, reimbursement should be provided regardless of whether an APN is associated with or practices under the supervision or direction of another health care provider.

In the 105th Congress, bills were introduced in both the House and Senate to provide Medicaid reimbursement directly to all NPs and CNSs regardless of geographic location or practice setting. Each of those bills had strong bipartisan support and will be reintroduced in the 106th Congress.

5

Support for the Nurse as an Essential Provider

Antitrust Reform

ISSUE

Continued application and enforcement of antitrust laws to activities in the health care industry.

BACKGROUND

The Federal Trade Commission (FTC) and the Antitrust Division of the Department of Justice (DOJ) are charged with the enforcement of federal antitrust laws. These laws seek to protect the consumer by barring anticompetitive activities that lead to higher prices and lower quality. Some segments of the health care industry have sought exemptions or a relaxation of antitrust enforcement. For example, during the debate on health care reform in the 103rd Congress, physician groups sought an exemption to allow them to negotiate fees collectively without antitrust scrutiny and hospitals sought exemptions to or a relaxation of requirements regarding hospital merger activity.

In the 105th Congress, legislation was introduced that would have granted broad antitrust exemptions to health care providers. The result of this legislation would have been increased health care costs to consumers, and it would have allowed physicians to compete unfairly against other health care providers, such as nurses. Such legislation would have allowed physicians who are competitors to engage in activities such as coordinated pricing. Though this legislation was not enacted, similar proposals will be introduced in the 106th Congress.

The antitrust laws have benefited the health care consumer. Under the antitrust laws, it is illegal for competitors to get together to discuss pricing or certain other business issues. This is intended to protect consumers from becoming victims of collusion designed to undermine competition. In addition, it protects other competitors who may not be included in the collusion. The FTC and DOJ have shown a willingness to be flexible, where appropriate, in the application of antitrust laws in order to address special problems such as the needs of rural health care consumers. This approach has proved to be a better alternative than the wholesale rewriting of the antitrust laws.

ANA POSITION

ANA opposes any erosion of the FTC or DOJ authority to scrutinize the business practices of health care providers and practitioners. ANA opposes legislation that would exempt physicians from many of the antitrust laws because it would result in increased costs for health care consumers and would allow physicians to compete unfairly against other health care providers, including nurses.

Barriers to Nursing Practice

ISSUE

Removal of barriers and discriminatory practices that interfere with full participation by nurses in the health care delivery system.

BACKGROUND

Although the Balanced Budget Act of 1997 (Public Law 105-33) did include antidiscriminatory language prohibiting Medicare + Choice plans from discriminating against health care professionals based on the license of the provider, the actual effect of that prohibition has not been demonstrated in the regulatory process. Many health plans continue to limit the number and type of participating providers and to exclude nurse providers and other types of health professionals, even though they offer quality, cost-effective care.

State licensure laws often prevent nurses and other health care professionals from functioning as substitutes for physicians in many situations where more than one type of health care professional could treat the patient. This is particularly true for primary care services, despite the fact that studies have concluded that much of the primary care delivered by physicians could be delivered as effectively and more economically by nurse practitioners (NPs). State licensure laws also govern whether an advanced practice nurse (APN) may prescribe medications. In addition, most require the supervision or collaboration of a physician, which increases patients' or other payers' expenses without necessarily adding any value.

ANA POSITION

The removal of arbitrary practice restrictions is crucial to achieving universal access to and coverage (payment) of health care services. The full participation of registered nurses (RNs) in the health care system will make access to health care affordable, available, acceptable, and accountable.

ANA supports legislation that prohibits discrimination by individual health plans, including fee-for-service arrangements, preferred provider organizations (PPOs), and health maintenance organizations (HMOs), based on the type, license, class, or specialty of a health care provider. Health plans must be required to make public, in advance, the criteria used to select participating providers and must have a sufficient mix of providers to ensure enrollees adequate access to covered services. States must not have the authority to impose on any class of health care professionals arbitrary practice restrictions that are not based on the licensure of those professionals. Specific language should direct states to eliminate practices that prevent RNs from delivering health care within the scope of their education, abilities, and competence. These barriers include state laws and regulations that limit or prohibit prescriptive authority, require supervision by or collaboration with another health care provider, limit direct reimbursement, prohibit or limit institutional privileges, and make it difficult to obtain liability insurance.

Graduate Nursing Education

ISSUE

Preparation of all health care professionals to deliver essential primary care services, as the health care delivery system continues to evolve.

BACKGROUND

Since its inception in 1965, the Medicare program has paid a portion of the costs of training health care professionals. Graduate Medical Education (GME) expenditures for nursing education are intended to reimburse a portion of the costs of nursing education to promote quality inpatient care for Medicare beneficiaries. Therefore, Medicare has traditionally made payments to hospitals for the "training" of nurses in hospital-based nurse education programs. A majority of these programs are hospital-based programs that grant a diploma rather than a bachelor of science (BSN) degree, which is granted by most university-based nursing education programs, or an associate degree granted by community colleges. Medicare reimburses hospitals based on a formula of payment for a portion of the cost of these hospital-operated nurse education programs, including classroom and clinical training. In 1997 Medicare provided approximately $290 million to hospitals in support of nursing education costs; 112 hospital diploma programs received the majority of this Medicare GME funding.

Since the enactment of Medicare, dramatic changes have occurred in nursing education. The locus of educational control has shifted from hospitals to educational institutions that grant four- and six-year degrees. For the most part, hospital-based nursing programs do not produce primary care providers. Primary care practitioners usually graduate from four-year programs and advanced nursing educational programs. Therefore, nursing finds that the primary federal support for nursing education is based on an outmoded system that reimburses nurse education programs that are least likely to be able to meet the growing need for primary care and community-based health care providers.

ANA POSITION

ANA believes that Medicare funds currently used for educational programs culminating in a diploma should be redirected on a phased-in basis to educate APNs. A graduate nurse education program would expand opportunities for professional registered nurses (RNs) to access programs that lead to a full complement of advanced practice capabilities. Because there is a continuing need for BSN-prepared nurses to play a variety of roles in the health care system, ANA also believes that current Medicare funds that reimburse hospitals for those programs should be maintained. In addition, ANA believes that funding must be available to the "RN-to-MSN" bridge programs. These are accelerated nursing education programs that enable diploma or associate degree nurses to become masters in a consolidated time frame and hence better able to meet the health care needs of the nation.

Nursing Education

ISSUE

Adequate appropriations funding for all federal nursing education programs.

BACKGROUND

In October 1992, the Health Professions Education Extension Amendments of 1992 reauthorized the largest federal nursing education program, generically called the Nurse Education Act (NEA). This legislation, which had strong bipartisan support, was reauthorized again for five years in the 105th Congress as the Health Professions Partnership Act of 1998 (Public Law 105-392). The act amended the Public Health Service Act to consolidate and restructure this program to allow for more efficient, flexible, and comprehensive federal financial support for nursing workforce development.

The Division of Nursing (DON), Bureau of Health Professions, Health Resources and Services Administration in the U.S. Public Health Service implements the NEA. The DON administers programs for advanced nursing education, nurse practitioner/nurse midwifery, nursing education opportunities for individuals from disadvantaged backgrounds, trainee opportunities for the advanced education of professional nurses, nurse anesthetist programs, the nurse loan repayment program, and the nursing student loan fund. Additional priorities include expanding enrollment in nursing programs, promoting career mobility programs, supporting continuing education programs for nurses in rural or underserved areas, and developing programs that expand access to primary care in underserved or rural communities. During the 105th Congress, NEA programs received support from both the administration and Congress and an appropriation of $67.8 million for fiscal year 1999.

Other federal nursing education support is incorporated in legislation and appropriations for several agencies, including the Department of Defense, Department of Veterans Affairs, Indian Health Service, Department of Agriculture, Disadvantaged and Minority Health Act programs, and others.

ANA POSITION

ANA believes that continued federal support for nursing education and research is essential to ensure sufficient numbers of nurses qualified to provide a full range of nursing services in all geographic areas. ANA supports increased funding for NEA and other federal programs that support nursing students and nursing programs. In addition, DON serves as the principal advisor to the Secretary of Health and Human Services for nursing affairs. It is important to preserve that function, as well as the data-analytic function that DON carries out. DON is the only entity with sufficient size and resources to perform significant analytic work on the entire workforce of nurses and other nursing personnel.

Nursing Research

ISSUE

Substantially increased funding for the National Institute of Nursing Research (NINR) at the National Institutes of Health (NIH).

BACKGROUND

The NINR conducts research on the care of individuals across the life span. Nursing research in the biomedical community brings a unique focus on the interrelationships of the behavioral and biological events that result in illness and resilience to illness.

NINR-supported nursing research provides a scientific base for patient care and is used by many disciplines, especially the nation's 2.6 million nurses. NINR-supported research is not disease specific, nor is it dedicated to a particular age group or population. Nursing research addresses the issues that examine the core of patients' and families' personal encounters with illness, treatment, and disease prevention. NINR's primary activity is clinical research, and most of the studies supported involve patients.

NINR receives the second lowest amount of funding from NIH. There is growing concern that this funding level limits NINR's ability to adequately support research and training. With a funding level of $69.8 million in fiscal year 1999, NINR was able to fund only 20 percent of its peer-reviewed, approved applications. The NIH average funding rate for peer-reviewed programs is about 28 percent.

ANA POSITION

ANA believes that research supported by NINR is driven by real and immediate problems encountered by patients and families. Study results offer the clear prospect of improving health, reducing morbidity and mortality, and lowering costs and demand for health care. ANA believes that NINR, as the focal point for the development, conduct, and support of biomedical and behavioral research and research training programs regarding nursing practice, must have adequate resources to meet its research needs. ANA supports advocating for a substantial increase in funding for NINR.

6

Workplace Environment and Safety

Employee Participation Committees

ISSUE

Use of employee participation committees in the workplace.

BACKGROUND

Since the 1980s, employers have sought increasingly to create employee participation and workplace committees as a mechanism to enhance quality, productivity, and employee satisfaction. The potential problems are whether such committees discuss interrelated issues of working conditions and how to share the gains produced by employee involvement, which traditionally have been elements negotiated under a collective bargaining agreement. In addition, some programs blur the distinction between supervisors or managers and workers. Formation of employee participation committees has been interpreted as a mechanism to bypass union organization or to create "sham unions" while management maintains complete authority over who participates on the committee and retains the ultimate decision-making authority.

The National Labor Relations Act (NLRA) defines a labor organization as "any organization of any kind, or any agency or employee representation committee or plan, in which employees participate and which exists for the purpose, in whole or in part, of dealing with employers concerning grievances, labor disputes . . . or conditions of work." Historically, Congress has considered the pressure of employer-dominated committees to unduly influence employees in their judgment regarding union representation. Section 8(a)(2) of the NLRA states that it is an unfair labor practice to dominate or interfere with the formation or administration of a labor organization. Congress is now under strong pressure by business interests to broaden the interpretation of Section 8(a)(2) to make it easier for employers to create such committees.

ANA POSITION

ANA believes that passage of any measure to more broadly interpret Section 8(a)(2) of the NLRA is a fundamental shift away from the rights of employees to choose independent representation and truly participate in improving the American workplace.

ANA supports cooperation between employees and employers through committee participation when there is true representation, such as when the employee representatives are elected union officers, the agenda is mutually chosen, and there is open and full discussion between equal partners.

Section 8(a)(2) of the NLRA was passed to guarantee employees complete discretion in designating representatives of their own choice without employer interference. This protection is fundamental to preventing employers from interfering with the legitimate efforts of workers to achieve a true independent voice.

National Labor Relations Board v. Healthcare and Retirement Corporation of America

ISSUE

Federal labor law protection for nurses who direct the work of others as part of their duties.

BACKGROUND

The *National Labor Relations Board (NLRB) v. Health Care and Retirement Corporation of America* involved three licensed practical nurses (LPNs) at the Heartland Nursing Home in Urbana, Ohio, who were fired for taking their complaints about working conditions to the nursing home management.

On May 23, 1994, the Supreme Court ruled that nurses who direct the work of others may be considered supervisors and thus are not protected by the National Labor Relations Act (NLRA). The case involved the analysis used by the NLRB to evaluate whether nurses are supervisors. The NLRA defines a supervisor as "any individual having authority, in the interest of the employer, to hire, transfer, suspend, lay off, recall, promote, discharge, assign, reward, or discipline other employees, or responsibly to direct them." Since 1974, the NLRB has analyzed cases involving the supervisory status of nurses and found that a "nurses's direction of less-skilled employees, in the exercise of professional judgment incidental to the treatment of patients, is not authority exercised in the interest of the employer."

In the majority opinion, the court rejected the NLRB's argument that nurses' direction of others is in the interest of patient care and is not authority exercised in the interest of the employer. The majority found that the LPNs "responsibly directed" the work of nurses' aides in a manner that used independent judgment and was done in the interest of the employer. In the dissenting opinion, Justice Ginsburg wrote that most professionals have some supervisory responsibilities in the sense that they direct another's work; given this ruling, few professionals would be covered by the NLRA. This ruling is contrary to the intent of Congress when it amended the Act to include professional employees.

ANA POSITION

The impact of this decision applies to all nurses in private health care settings. The NLRA protects any concerted or group employee activity related to terms and conditions of employment, including signing petitions, sending letters, holding meetings or organized discussions, or airing grievances. This decision also poses a direct threat to a nurse's ability to carry out her or his long-standing ethical and legal obligation to serve as patient advocates.

ANA considers this ruling a serious threat to nurses' protection under national labor laws to act together to improve working conditions. ANA believes that, under the NLRA, directing the work of less-skilled employees is part of the nurse's professional duties, and not supervision.

Nursing and Patient Safety

ISSUE

Replacement of registered nurses (RNs) with unlicensed workers.

BACKGROUND

The hospital industry is in a state of massive restructuring. Hospitals are changing the way they operate, the way care is delivered, and the way their employees are utilized. Many hospitals and other health care institutions employ fewer RNs to provide direct patient care, choosing instead to replace nurses with minimally trained, unlicensed personnel.

In response to these changes, ANA drafted legislation, The Patient Safety Act, as a component of its Every Patient Deserves a Nurse campaign. The legislation focuses on major safety, quality, and workforce issues for nurses employed by health care institutions and patients who receive care in those institutions. This legislation, which has been introduced in the 104th, 105th, and 106th Congresses, would

- Require all health care institutions to make public specific information regarding staffing levels and mix, and patient outcomes (e.g., the number of RNs providing direct care, the number of unlicensed personnel utilized to provide direct patient care, the average number of patients per RN providing direct patient care, and patient mortality rates).
- Add whistle-blower language to the Medicare law to protect health care workers who report or voice concerns about unsafe working conditions; a violation of this provision would make an institution ineligible for Medicare participation.
- Authorize the Secretary of the Department of Health and Human Services (DHHS) to review mergers and acquisitions of health care institutions to ensure that community health and access needs are not compromised.

The introduction of the Patient Safety Act and ANA's lobbying efforts and grassroots activities in support of the bill have led to an increased awareness among policymakers of the growing trend to reduce RN staffing in hospitals and the impact this trend has on the safety and quality of care.

ANA POSITION

ANA strongly supports the Patient Safety Act and other efforts that ensure that patients receive safe, quality nursing care in hospitals and other health care institutions. ANA believes that one of the most reliable and cost-effective ways to ensure quality is to have RNs at the bedside.

Occupational Safety and Health

ISSUE

Federal laws and regulations that provide health and safety hazard prevention for health care workers.

BACKGROUND

Health care is a hazardous occupation. The rate of injury and illness to health care workers, including registered nurses (RNs), has been on the rise since 1982. In 1991, the rate of injury and illness among health care workers surpassed that of general industry. In fact, the rate of injuries among nursing home workers has exceeded that of construction workers.

The Occupational Safety and Health Administration (OSHA) has set the following rulemaking priorities relevant to nursing:

- Respiratory protections;
- Recording and reporting of occupational injuries and illnesses;
- Prevention of work-related musculoskeletal disorders, occupational exposure to tuberculosis, and latex allergy;
- Indoor air quality;
- Permissible exposure limits for air contaminants such as glutaraldehyde; and
- Recording of needle-stick injuries in the OSHA 200 log.

ANA POSITION

ANA opposes any efforts to weaken OSHA and its efforts to protect workers. ANA supports increased research of occupational health and safety hazards in health care facilities and the development of guidelines and standards to reduce employee exposures. ANA supports legislation expanding education and training of health care workers regarding hazards and protective measures. The number of needle-stick injuries suffered by health care workers has increased dramatically in recent years. ANA supports OSHA's efforts to include needle-stick injuries in the OSHA 200 log and their research into a possible needle-stick directive. ANA supports federal legislation that mandates safer needle-stick devices in all health care settings.

ANA's safety and health agenda includes work on the health and safety effects of

- Restructuring;
- Indoor air quality, including latex allergy and the release of smoke plumes as the result of using lasers;
- Continued enforcement of the bloodborne pathogen standard and increased utilization of needleless systems;
- Ergonomics studies; and
- Prevention measures and education related to violence in the workplace.

Whistle-Blowing

ISSUE

Protection of nurses' right to speak out about activities or practices that threaten the health and safety of the public or the environment.

BACKGROUND

Whistle-blowing is the public disclosure of unlawful or hazardous activities or practices by members of one's own organization. This action often occurs after employees have exhausted existing channels for correcting problems, or when employers are unresponsive or have retaliated in the past.

Whistle-blowing by nurses usually results from concern about issues that jeopardize the health or safety of patients or occupational safety and health violations that place the employee at risk. Although they are responsible for patient care and well-being, nurses often are powerless when another health care provider performs unethical or life-threatening practices. There have been a number of legal cases involving nurses who have "blown the whistle" on their employers. In particular, nurses have been instrumental in identifying violations of research standards and refusal of care to newborns.

In 1989 Congress enacted the Whistle-Blower Protection Act to protect federal workers. This law was expanded in 1994 to cover workers in veterans' facilities hired under Title 38, as well as government corporation employees. However, current whistle-blowing laws remain a patchwork of incomplete coverage. Fear of reprisal and lack of protection prevent many employees from taking the risk of trying to protect public health and safety. Reprisal may include dismissal, harassment, or blacklisting.

ANA POSITION

ANA has drafted model language in the Patient Safety Act that adds whistle-blower protections to the Medicare law. Health care institutions that violate this protection would be ineligible to participate in the Medicare program for a specified period of time. ANA also has advocated for whistle-blower protection in the Patients' Bill of Rights.

Nurses are ethically obligated to advocate on behalf of their patients. Yet they have voiced strong concern about retaliation from their employers when they speak out about dangerous patient care conditions. Any barriers to nurses' ability to protect their patients must be removed. Nurses need clear and explicit whistle-blower protections.

Appendixes

Appendix A. Abbreviations and Acronyms

AHCPR	Agency for Health Care Policy and Research
AIDS	acquired immune deficiency syndrome
ANA-PAC	American Nurses Association Political Action Committee
APN	advanced practice nurse
ATF	Bureau of Alcohol, Tobacco, and Firearms
BSN	Bachelor of Science, Nursing
CDC	Centers for Disease Control and Prevention
CGFNS	Commission on Graduates of Foreign Nursing Schools
CHAMPUS	Civilian Health and Medical Programs of the United States
CNM	certified nurse midwife
CNO	Community Nursing Organization
CNS	clinical nurse specialist
COGME	Council on Graduate Medical Education
CRNA	certified registered nurse anesthetist
DEA	Drug Enforcement Administration
DHHS	Department of Health and Human Services
DOD	Department of Defense
DOJ	Department of Justice
DOL	Department of Labor
DON	Division of Nursing
DVA	Department of Veterans Affairs
ERISA	Employee Retirement Income Security Act
FLSA	Fair Labor Standards Act
FNP	family nurse practitioner
FTC	Federal Trade Commission
GAO	General Accounting Office
GATT	General Agreement on Tariffs and Trades
GME	graduate medical education
HCFA	Health Care Financing Administration
HIPAA	Health Insurance Portability and Accountability Act of 1996
HIV	human immunodeficiency virus
HMO	health maintenance organization
IHS	Indian Health Service
INS	Immigration and Naturalization Service
IOM	Institute of Medicine
LPN	licensed practical nurse

MedPAC	Medicare Payment Advisory Commission (formed by consolidating PPRC and ProPAC)
MEWA	Multiple Employer Welfare Arrangements
MSN	Master of Science, Nursing
NAFTA	North American Free Trade Agreement
NEA	Nurse Education Act
NIH	National Institutes of Health
NINR	National Institute of Nursing Research
NIOSH	National Institute of Occupational Safety and Health
NLRA	National Labor Relations Act
NLRB	National Labor Relations Board
NORA	National Occupational Research Agenda
NP	nurse practitioner
N-STAT	Nurses Strategic Action Team
OBRA	Omnibus Budget Reconciliation Act
OSHA	Occupational Safety and Health Administration
PAC	political action committee
PHS	Public Health Service
PNP	pediatric nurse practitioner
PPS	prospective payment system
PPO	preferred provider organization
RN	registered nurse
SNA	state nurses association
UNAIDS	Joint United Nations Programme on HIV/AIDS
VAWA	Violence Against Women Act
VAWAII	Violence Against Women Act II
WHO	World Health Organization

Appendix B. How to Obtain Government Documents

HARD COPY

Copies of public laws and House or Senate bills can be obtained from the respective document room noted below. Request only one copy of each bill or federal law and enclose a peel-off label with your name and address for the staff to use on the return envelope. There is no charge for most bills.

One copy of no more than six different items (bills, committee reports, public laws) may be requested in writing daily from the Senate Document Room and one copy of no more than 12 different items may be requested in writing daily from the House Legislative Resource Center.

Facsimile and telephone requests are not recommended.

Senate Document Room
SH-B04 Hart Senate Office Building
Washington, DC 20510-7106
202-224-7860

House Legislative Resource Center
B106 Cannon H.O.B.
Washington, DC 20515
202-226-5200

ON-LINE INFORMATION

Sites, or "pages," on the World Wide Web are often the fastest way to get information from the government. The amount of information available to anyone with Internet access is truly amazing. Virtually all government agencies have web sites. You often can download or print out documents, including everything from government regulations to job applications and tax forms, from various web pages. It is likely that the Internet will be used more and more in the future as a method of making government information widely and easily available.

The U.S. Congress maintains several sites. The main site for legislative information is "Thomas" maintained by the Library of Congress at http://thomas.loc.gov. Thomas has information about the status of legislation, the legislative process, and the legislative schedule. You can download or print copies of House and Senate bills. In addition, the House and Senate each have their own web sites. The House site is at www.house.gov and the Senate site is at www.senate.gov. The House and Senate sites have information about how to contact individual members as well as committee schedules and other information. You also can send e-mail messages to members of the House or Senate on these web pages. In addition, the Clerk of the House maintains a site at clerkweb.house.gov that contains legislative information.

The White House has a web site at www.whitehouse.gov that includes speeches from the President and a great deal of other information. You also can use this web page to send e-mail to the President or Vice President.

The Government Printing Office (GPO) maintains an extensive web site called GPO ACCESS at www.access.gpo.gov (with a mirror site at www.gpo.gov). You can access or search many government documents using this site, including the U.S. Code, the Code of Federal Regulations, bills pending in Congress, and much more.

You also can get a lot of valuable information from the sites of individual government agencies. It's usually easy to find the web page for a given agency. For instance, the Health Care Financing Administration (HCFA), the agency that administers Medicare and Medicaid, has its web site at www.hcfa.gov. The Agency for Health Care Policy and Research (AHCPR) is at www.ahcpr.gov. Some of the agency sites are better than others, but most agencies are putting more and more information on their web pages so it's worth checking back from time to time.

INFORMATION ON CD-ROM

Computer diskettes and compact disks with read-only-memory (CD-ROMs) that contain the text of federal regulations and other federal data are available in most public libraries. Some diskettes and CD-ROMs are produced by commercial enterprises. Others are produced under contract or license from the federal government and are made available at no or low cost.

The U.S. Code is available on CD-ROM from the GPO. Federal acquisition regulations and federal information on resources management regulations also are available on CD-ROM. HCFA laws, regulations, and manuals also are available in CD-ROM format, as are OSHA regulations, documents, and technical information.

Appendix C. Index of ANA Positions on Legislative and Regulatory Initiatives for the 106th Congress

Appendix D. Important Phone Numbers and Listings

The White House

1600 Pennsylvania Avenue, NW
Washington, DC 20500
Phone: 202-456-1414

Office of the President
William J. Clinton 202-456-1414

Office of the Vice President
Albert Gore, Jr. 202-456-2326
Chief of Staff–Ron Klain 202-456-6605

Office of Chief of Staff
John Podesta 202-456-6798

Office of the First Lady
Hillary Rodham Clinton 202-456-6266

Executive Offices of the President
White House Management and
  Administration–Virginia A. Apuzzo 202-456-2861
Cabinet Affairs–Thurgood Marshall, Jr. 202-456-2572
Central Intelligence Agency–George Tenet .. 703-482-6363
Communications Director–Ann F. Lewis 202-456-2640

Counsel to the President–Charles Ruff 202-456-2632
Counselor to the President– 202-456-1125
Domestic Policy Council–Bruce Reed 202-456-2216
Intergovernmental Affairs–Mickey Ibarra ... 202-456-7060
Legislative Affairs–Larry Stein 202-456-2230
Management and Budget–Jacob J. Lew 202-456-4840
Military Office–Joseph J. Simmons IV 202-456-2150
National Economic Council–Gene Sperling .. 202-456-2620
National Security Council–Samuel Berger 202-456-9481
Policy Development– 202-456-6406
Policy and Strategy–Doug Sosnik 202-456-1290
Political Affairs–Minyon Moore 202-456-1125
Presidential Scheduling and Advance–
  Dan Rosenthal (Advance) 202-456-5327
  Stephanie Streett (Scheduling) 202-456-7560
Presidential Personnel–Robert Nash 202-456-6676
Press Secretary–Joe Lockhart 202-456-2673
Public Liaison–Ben Johnson 202-456-2930
Science and Technology Policy–Neal Lane ... 202-456-7116
U.S. Trade Representative–Charlene Barshefsky 202-395-6890

The Cabinet

Department of Agriculture 202-720-3631
14th Street and Independence Avenue, SW
Washington, DC 20250

Department of Commerce 202-482-2112
14th Street and Constitution Avenue, NW
Washington, DC 20230

Department of Defense 703-695-5261
The Pentagon, 1000 Defense
Washington, DC 20301-1000

Department of Education 202-401-3000
400 Maryland Avenue, SW
Washington, DC 20202

Department of Energy 202-586-6210
1000 Independence Avenue, SW
Washington, DC 20585

Department of Health and Human Services 202-690-7000
200 Independence Avenue, SW
Washington, DC 20201

Department of Housing and
  Urban Development 202-708-0417
451 7th Street, SW
Washington, DC 20410

Department of Interior 202-208-7351
1849 C Street, NW
Washington, DC 20240

Department of Justice 202-514-2001
950 Pennsylvania Avenue, NW
Washington, DC 20530

Department of Labor 202-219-8271
200 Constitution Avenue, NW
Washington, DC 20210

Department of State 202-647-4000
2201 C Street, NW
Washington, DC 20520

Department of Transportation 202-366-1111
400 7th Street, NW
Washington, DC 20590

Department of the Treasury 202-622-5300
1500 Pennsylvania Avenue, NW
Washington, DC 20220

Department of Veterans Affairs 202-273-4800
810 Vermont Avenue, NW
Washington, DC 20420

The Supreme Court

United States Supreme Court Building
1 First Street, NE
Washington, DC 20543
Phone: 202-479-3000

Chief Justice
William H. Rehnquist

Associate Justices
John Paul Stevens
Sandra Day O'Connor
Antonin Scalia
Anthony M. Kennedy
David H. Souter
Clarence Thomas
Ruth Bader Ginsburg
Stephen Breyer

Selected Agencies

Commission on Civil Rights   202-376-8312
624 9th Street, NW
Washington, DC 20425

Consumer Product Safety Commission   301-504-0990
4330 East West Highway
Bethesda, Maryland 20207

Drug Enforcement Administration   202-307-7363
700 Army-Navy Drive
Arlington, Virginia 22202

Equal Employment Opportunity Commission   202-663-4900
1801 L Street, NW
Washington, DC 20507

Federal Elections Commission   800-424-9530
999 E Street, NW
Washington, DC 20463

Food and Drug Administration   301-443-1544
5600 Fishers Lane, Room 15A-07
Rockville, Maryland 20857

Government Printing Office   202-512-1993
732 North Capitol Street, NW
Washington, DC 20401

Health Care Financing Administration   202-690-6726
200 Independence Avenue, SW
Washington, DC 20201

Immigration and Naturalization Service   202-514-5231
425 Eye Street, NW
Washington, DC 20536

Internal Revenue Service   202-662-4010
1111 Constitution Avenue, NW
Washington, DC 20224

International Trade Commission   202-205-2000
500 E Street, SW
Washington, DC 20436

National Institutes of Health   301-496-4461
9000 Rockville Pike, #344 Building 1
Bethesda, Maryland 20892

National Science Foundation   703-306-1070
4201 Wilson Boulevard, #1245
Arlington, Virginia 22230

Occupational Safety and Health Administration 202-693-2000
200 Constitution Avenue, NW
Washington, DC 20210

Office of Personnel Management   202-606-1800
1900 E Street, NW
Washington, DC 20415

Small Business Administration   202-205-6600
409 Third Street, SW
Washington, DC 20416

Smithsonian Institution   202-357-2627
1000 Jefferson Drive, SW
Washington, DC 20560

Social Security Administration   410-965-1720
6401 Security Boulevard
Baltimore, Maryland 21235

Surgeon General   301-443-6496
Parklawn Building
5600 Fishers Lane, Room 18-66
Rockville, Maryland 20857

U.S. Customs Service   202-927-1770
1301 Pennsylvania Avenue, NW
Washington, DC 20229

U.S. Postal Service   202-268-2000
475 L'Enfant Plaza, SW
Washington, DC 20260

Useful Federal Government Information

Area code is 202 unless otherwise indicated.

U.S. CONGRESS
U.S. Capitol Switchboard

To obtain telephone numbers for Senate offices   224-3121
To obtain telephone numbers for House offices   225-3121

Senate Democratic Cloakroom
  Tape of floor action and scheduling information   224-8541

Senate Republican Cloakroom
Tape of floor action and scheduling information 224-8601
House Democratic Cloakroom
Tape of floor action and scheduling information 225-7400

House Republican Cloakroom
Tape of floor action and scheduling information 225-7430
House and Senate Legislative Information (LEGIS)
Status of bills 225-1772

EXECUTIVE BRANCH AND SELECTED WASHINGTON NUMBERS

The White House	456-1414
Office of the President	456-2168
Office of the Vice President	224-2326
Department of Health and Human Services	690-7000
Department of Labor, Public Information	219-7316
Food and Drug Administration	301-443-2410
Government Printing Office,	
Publications and Orders	783-3238

Health Care Financing Administration	
Public Affairs	690-6113
Medicare Hotline	1-800-638-6833
Provider Services	410-966-5661
Library of Congress	707-5000
Reference	707-5522
National Institutes of Health	301-496-4000
National Institute of Nursing Research	301-496-0207

Senate Leadership

Area code is 202 for all numbers.

President
Albert Gore, Jr.
Vice President of the United States
Deputy Counsel and Director to the Vice President for
   Legislative Affairs: Kay Casstevens
Office: S-212
Phone: 224-2424

President Pro Tempore
Strom Thurmond (R-SC)
Office: SR-237
Phone: 224-6233

Majority Leader
Trent Lott (R-MS)
Chief of Staff: Dave Hoppe
Office: S-230
Phone: 224-3135

Assistant Majority Leader
Don Nickles (R-OK)
Chief of Staff: Eric Ueland
Office: S-208
Phone: 224-2708

Rep. Policy Committee Chair
Larry Craig (R-ID)
Staff Director: Jade West
Office: SR-347
Phone: 224-3347

Rep. Conference Chairman
Connie Mack (R-FL)
Staff Director: Mark Mills
Office: SH-405
Phone: 224-2764

Democrat Conference Chairman/Minority Leader
Thomas A. Daschle (D-SD)
Chief of Staff: Pete Rouse
Office: S-221
Phone: 224-5556

Minority Whip
Harry Reid (D-NV)
Staff Director: Susan McCue
Office: S-148
Phone: 224-2158

Democrat Policy Committee Chair
Thomas A. Daschle (D-SD)
Staff Director: Joel Johnson
Office: SH-419
Phone: 224-3232

Secretary of Senate
Gary Sisco
Administrative Assistant: Jon Lynn Kerchner
Office: S-220
Phone: 224-1622

Sergeant at Arms
James W. Ziglar
Office: S-321
Phone: 224-2341

Majority Secretary
Elizabeth Letchworth
Office: S-337
Phone: 224-3835

Minority Secretary
Marty Paone
Office: S-309
Phone: 224-3735

Parliamentarian
Robert Dove
Office: S-133
Phone: 224-6128

Assistant Secretary
Sharon Zelaska
Office: S-312
Phone: 224-2114

Chaplain
Rev. and Dr. Lloyd Ogilvie
Office: SR-325B
Phone: 224-2510

Senators, Alphabetical Listing

SD - Senate Dirksen Office Building
SH - Senate Hart Office Building
SR - Senate Russell Office Building
Area code is 202 for all numbers.

Abraham, Spencer (R-MI)	SD-329	224-4822
Akaka, Daniel (D-HI)	SH-720	224-6361
Allard, Wayne (R-CO)	SH-513	224-5941
Ashcroft, John (R-MO)	SH-316	224-6154
Baucus, Max (D-MT)	SH-511	224-2651
Bayh, Evan (D-IN)	SH-717	224-5623
Bennett, Robert (R-UT)	SD-431	224-5444
Biden, Joseph Jr. (D-DE)	SR-221	224-5042
Bingaman, Jeff (D-NM)	SH-703	224-5521
Bond, Christopher (R-MO)	SR-274	224-5721
Boxer, Barbara (D-CA)	SH-112	224-3553
Breaux, John (D-LA)	SH-503	224-4623
Brownback, Sam (R-KS)	SH-303	224-6521
Bryan, Richard H. (D-NV)	SR-269	224-6244
Bunning, Jim (R-KY)	SH-502	224-4343
Burns, Conrad (R-MT)	SD-187	224-2644
Byrd, Robert (D-WV)	SH-311	224-3954
Campbell, Ben Nighthorse (R-CO)	SR-380	224-5852
Chafee, John (R-RI)	SD-505	224-2921
Cleland, Max (D-GA)	SD-461	224-3521
Cochran, Thad (R-MS)	SR-326	224-5054
Collins, Susan (R-ME)	SR-172	224-2523
Conrad, Kent (D-ND)	SH-530	224-2043
Coverdell, Paul (R-GA)	SR-200	224-3643
Craig, Larry (R-ID)	SH-520	224-2752
Crapo, Mike (R-ID)	SR-111	224-6142
Daschle, Thomas (D-SD)	SH-509	224-2321
DeWine, Mike (R-OH)	SR-140	224-2315
Dodd, Christopher (D-CT)	SR-444	224-2823
Domenici, Pete (R-NM)	SH-328	224-6621
Dorgan, Byron (D-ND)	SH-714	224-2551
Durbin, Richard (D-IL)	SR-364	224-2152
Edwards, John (D-NC)	SH-825	224-3154
Enzi, Mike (R-WY)	SR-290	224-3424
Feingold, Russ (D-WI)	SH-716	224-5323
Feinstein, Dianne (D-CA)	SH-331	224-3841
Fitzgerald, Peter (R-IL)	SD-555	224-2854
Frist, William (R-TN)	SR-416	224-3344
Gorton, Slade (R-WA)	SH-730	224-3441
Graham, Bob (D-FL)	SH-524	224-3041
Gramm, Phil (R-TX)	SR-370	224-2934
Grams, Rod (R-MN)	SD-257	224-3244
Grassley, Charles (R-IA)	SH-135	224-3744
Gregg, Judd (R-NH)	SR-393	224-3324
Hagel, Charles (R-NE)	SR-346	224-4224
Harkin, Tom (D-IA)	SH-731	224-3254
Hatch, Orrin (R-UT)	SR-131	224-5251
Helms, Jesse (R-NC)	SD-403	224-6342
Hollings, Ernest (D-SC)	SR-125	224-6121
Hutchinson, Tim (R-AR)	SD-245	224-2353
Hutchison, Kay Bailey (R-TX)	SR-284	224-5922
Inhofe, James (R-OK)	SR-453	224-4721
Inouye, Daniel (D-HI)	SH-722	224-3934
Jeffords, James (R-VT)	SH-728	224-5141
Johnson, Tim (D-SD)	SH-324	224-5842
Kennedy, Edward (D-MA)	SR-315	224-4543
Kerrey, Robert (D-NE)	SH-141	224-6551
Kerry, John (D-MA)	SR-304	224-2742
Kohl, Herbert (D-WI)	SH-330	224-5653
Kyl, Jon (R-AZ)	SH-724	224-4521
Landrieu, Mary (D-LA)	SH-702	224-5824
Lautenberg, Frank (D-NJ)	SH-506	224-4744
Leahy, Patrick (D-VT)	SR-433	224-4242
Levin, Carl (D-MI)	SR-459	224-6221
Lieberman, Joseph (D-CT)	SH-706	224-4041
Lincoln, Blanche (D-AR)	SD-359	224-4843
Lott, Trent (R-MS)	SR-487	224-6253
Lugar, Richard (R-IN)	SH-306	224-4814
Mack, Connie (R-FL)	SH-517	224-5274
McCain, John (R-AZ)	SR-241	224-2235
McConnell, Mitch (R-KY)	SR-361A	224-2541
Mikulski, Barbara (D-MD)	SH-709	224-4654
Moynihan, Daniel Patrick (D-NY)	SR-464	224-4451
Murkowski, Frank (R-AK)	SH-322	224-6665
Murray, Patty (D-WA)	SR-173	224-2621
Nickles, Don (R-OK)	SH-133	224-5754
Reed, Jack (D-RI)	SH-320	224-4642
Reid, Harry (D-NV)	SH-528	224-3542
Robb, Charles (D-VA)	SR-154	224-4024
Roberts, Pat (R-KS)	SH-302	224-4774
Rockefeller, John IV (D-WV)	SH-531	224-6472
Roth, William Jr. (R-DE)	SH-104	224-2441
Santorum, Rick (R-PA)	SR-120	224-6324
Sarbanes, Paul (D-MD)	SH-309	224-4524
Schumer, Charles (D-NY)	SH-313	224-6542
Sessions, Jeff (R-AL)	SR-495	224-4124
Shelby, Richard (R-AL)	SH-110	224-5744
Smith, Bob (R-NH)	SD-307	224-2841
Smith, Gordon (R-OR)	SR-404	224-3753
Snowe, Olympia (R-ME)	SR-250	224-5344
Specter, Arlen (R-PA)	SH-711	224-4254
Stevens, Ted (R-AK)	SH-522	224-3004
Thomas, Craig (R-WY)	SH-109	224-6441
Thompson, Fred (R-TN)	SD-523	224-4944
Thurmond, Strom (R-SC)	SR-217	224-5972
Torricelli, Robert (D-NJ)	SD-113	224-3224
Voinovich, George (R-OH)	SH-317	224-3353
Warner, John (R-VA)	SR-225	224-2023
Wellstone, Paul (D-MN)	SH-136	224-5641
Wyden, Ron (D-OR)	SH-516	224-5244

Key Senate Committees

Area code is 202 for all numbers.

SENATE APPROPRIATIONS COMMITTEE
Phone: 224-3471
Room: S-128 Capitol

Republicans
Ted Stevens (AK), Chair
Thad Cochran (MS)
Arlen Specter (PA)
Pete V. Domenici (NM)
Christopher S. Bond (MO)
Slade Gorton (WA)
Mitch McConnell (KY)
Harry Reid (NV)
Richard C. Shelby (AL)
Judd Gregg (NH)
Robert Bennett (UT)
Ben Nighthorse Campbell (CO)
Larry E. Craig (ID)
Kay Bailey Hutchison (TX)
Jon L. Kyl (AZ)

Democrats
Robert C. Byrd (WV), Ranking Member
Daniel K. Inouye (HI)
Ernest F. Hollings (SC)
Patrick J. Leahy (VT)
Frank R. Lautenberg (NJ)
Tom Harkin (IA)
Barbara A. Mikulski (MD)
Herbert H. Kohl (WI)
Patty Murray (WA)
Bryon L. Dorgan (ND)
Dianne Feinstein (CA)
Richard J. Durbin (IL)

Majority Staff Director
Steve Cortese
224-3471, S-128 Capitol

Minority Staff Director
James English
224-7200, S-206 Capitol

Senate Appropriations Subcommittees

Agriculture, Rural Development, and Related Agencies
224-5270, SD-136
Republicans: Cochran, Chair; Specter; Bond; Gorton;
  McConnell; Burns
Democrats: Kohl, Ranking Member; Harkin; Dorgan;
  Feinstein; Durbin
Majority Staff Director: Rebecca Davies, 224-5270, SD-136
Minority Clerk: Galen Fountain, 224-7202, SH-123

Commerce, Justice, State, and Judiciary
224-7255, S-146A Capitol
Republicans: Gregg, Chair; Stevens; Domenici; McConnell;
  Hutchison; Campbell
Democrats: Hollings, Ranking Member; Inouye; Lautenberg;
  Mikulski; Leahy
Majority Staff Director: Jim Morhard, 224-727, S-146A
  Capitol
Minority Clerk: Lila Helms, 224-7270, SD-160

Defense
224-7277, SD-119
Republicans: Stevens, Chair; Cochran; Specter; Domenici;
  Bond; McConnell; Shelby; Gregg; Hutchison
Democrats: Inouye, Ranking Member; Hollings; Bryd; Leahy;
  Lautenberg; Harkin, Dorgan; Durbin
Majority Staff Director: Steve Cortese, 224-2739, SD-119
Minority Clerk: Charles Houy, 224-7293, SD-117

District of Columbia
224-3471, S-128 Capitol
Republicans: Hutchinson, Chair; Kyl
Democrats: Durbin, Ranking Member

Majority Staff Director: Mary Beth Nethercutt, 224-3471,
  SD-142
Minority Clerk: Terry Sauvain, 224-0338, SD-144

Energy and Water Development
224-7260, SD-127 Capitol
Republicans: Domenici, Chair; Cochran; Gorton;
  McConnell; Bennett; Burns; Craig
Democrats: Reid, Ranking Member; Byrd; Hollings; Murray;
  Kohl; Dorgan
Majority Staff Director: Alex Flint, 224-7260, SD-127
Minority Clerk: Greg Daines, 224-0335, SD-156

Foreign Operations
224-2104, SD-142
Republicans: McConnell, Chair; Specter; Gregg; Shelby;
  Bennett; Campbell; Bond
Democrats: Leahy, Ranking Member; Inouye; Lautenberg;
  Harkin; Mikulski; Murray
Majority Staff Director: Robin Cleveland, 224-2104, SD-142
Minority Clerk: Tim Reiser, 224-7284, SH-123

Interior
224-7233, SD-131
Republicans: Gorton, Chair; Stevens; Cochran; Domenici;
  Burns; Bennett; Gregg; Campbell
Democrats: Byrd, Ranking Member; Leahy; Bumpers;
  Hollings; Reid; Dorgan; Kohl; Feinstein
Majority Staff Director: Bruce Evans, 224-7262, SD-131
Minority Clerk: Kurt Dodd, 224-5271, SH-123

Labor, Health and Human Services, and Education
224-7230, SD-186
Republicans: Specter, Chair; Cochran; Gorton; Gregg; Craig; Hutchinson; Stevens; Kyl
Democrats: Harkin, Ranking Member; Hollings; Inouye; Reid; Kohl; Murray; Feinstein
Majority Staff Director: Bettilou Taylor, 224-7230, SD-186
Minority Clerk: Ellen Murray, 224-7288, SH-123

Legislative Branch
224-8921, S-125 Capitol
Republicans: Bennett, Chair; Stevens; Craig
Democrats: Feinstein, Ranking Member; Durbin
Majority Clerk: Christine Ciccone, 224-8921, S-125 Capitol
Minority Staff Director: James English, 224-7200, S-206 Capitol

Military Construction
224-3378, SD-140
Republicans: Burns, Chair; Hutchinson; Craig; Kyl
Democrats: Murray, Ranking Member; Reid; Inouye
Majority Staff Director: Sid Ashworth, 224-3378, SD-140
Minority Clerk: Christina Evans, 224-3088, SH-123

Transportation
224-7281, SD-133
Republicans: Shelby, Chair; Domenici; Specter; Bond; Gorton; Bennett; Campbell
Democrats: Lautenberg, Ranking Member; Byrd; Mikulski; Reid; Kohl; Murray
Majority Staff Director: Wally Burnett, 224-7281, SD-133
Minority Clerk: Peter Rogoff, 224-7245, SH-123

Treasury and General Government
224-7337, SD-190
Republicans: Campbell, Chair; Shelby; Kyl
Democrats: Dorgan, Ranking Member; Mikulski
Majority Clerk: Pat Raymond, 224-1394, SD-188
Minority Clerk: Barbara A. Retzlaff, 224-6280, SD-196

VA-HUD and Independent Agencies
224-7211, SD-127
Republicans: Bond, Chair; Burns; Shelby; Craig; Hutchinson; Kyl
Democrats: Mikulski, Ranking Member; Leahy; Lautenberg; Harkin; Byrd
Majority Staff Director: John Kamarck, 224-7211, SD-127
Minority Clerk: Andy Givens, 224-7231, SD-134

SENATE BUDGET COMMITTEE

Phone: 224-0642
Room: SD-621

Republicans
Pete V. Domenici (NM), Chair
Charles E. Grassley (IA)
Don Nickles (OK)
Phil Gramm (TX)
Christopher S. Bond (MO)
Slade Gorton (WA)
Judd Gregg (NH)
Olympia J. Snowe (ME)
Spencer Abraham (MI)
Bill Frist (TN)
Rod Grams (MN)
Gordon Smith (OR)

Majority Staff Director
G. William Hoagland
224-0769, SD-602

no subcommittees

Democrats
Frank R. Lautenberg (NJ), Ranking Member
Ernest F. Hollings (SC)
Kent Conrad (ND)
Paul S. Sarbanes (MD)
Barbara Boxer (CA)
Patty Murray (WA)
Ron Wyden (OR)
Russ Feingold (WI)
Tim Johnson (SD)
Richard J. Durbin (IL)

Minority Staff Director
Bruce King
224-0642, SD-634

SENATE COMMERCE, SCIENCE, AND TRANSPORTATION COMMITTEE

Phone: 224-5115
Room: SD-508

Republicans
John McCain (AZ), Chair
Ted Stevens (AK)
Conrad Burns (MT)
Slade Gorton (WA)
Trent Lott (MS)
Kay Bailey Hutchinson (TX)
Olympia J. Snowe (ME)
John Ashcroft (MO)
Bill Frist (TN)
Spencer Abraham (MI)
Sam Brownback (KS)

Democrats
Ernest F. Hollings (SC), Ranking Member
Daniel K. Inouye (HI)
John D. Rockefeller IV (WV)
John F. Kerry (MA)
John B. Breaux (LA)
Richard H. Bryan (NV)
Byron L. Dorgan (ND)
Ron Wyden (OR)
Max Cleland (GA)

Majority Staff Director
Mark Buse
224-1251, SR-254

Minority Staff Director/Chief Counsel
Ivan Schlager
224-0427, SD-558

Senate Commerce, Science, and Transportation Subcommittees

Aviation
224-4852, SH-427
Republicans: Gorton, Chair; Stevens; Burns; Lott;
Hutchinson; Ashcroft; Frist; Snowe; Brownback; Abraham
Democrats: Rockefeller, Ranking Member; Hollings; Inouye;
Bryan; Breaux; Dorgan; Wyden; Cleland
Majority Senior Counsel: Ann Choiniere, 224-4852, SH-427
Minority Professional Staff Member: Sam Whitehorn,
224-0411, SD-558

Communications
224-5184, SH-227
Republicans: Burns, Chair; Stevens; Gorton; Lott; Ashcroft;
Hutchinson; Abraham; First; Brownback
Democrats: Hollings, Ranking Member; Inouye; Kerry;
Breaux; Rockefeller; Dorgan; Wyden; Cleland
Majority Senior Counsel: Lauren "Pete" Belvin, 224-5184,
SH-227
Minority Senior Counsel: Paula Ford, 224-9340, SD-558

Consumer Affairs, Foreign Commerce, and Tourism
224-5183, SH-425
Republicans: Ashcroft, Chair; Gorton; Abraham; Burns;
Brownback
Democrats: Bryan, Ranking Member; Breaux
Majority Counsel: Lance Bultena, 224-5183, SH-425
Minority Senior Counsel: Moses Boyd, 224-0411, SD-558

Manufacturing and Competitiveness
224-1745, SR-254
Republicans: Abraham, Chair; Snowe; Ashcroft; Frist;
Brownback
Democrats: Dorgan, Ranking Member; Bryan; Hollings;
Rockefeller

Majority Senior Staff Member: Greg Willihauck, 224-1745,
RS-254
Minority Senior Staff Member: Gregg Elias, 224-0411,
SD-558

Oceans and Fisheries
224-8172, SH-428
Republicans: Snowe, Chair; Stevens; Gorton; Hutchinson
Democrats: Kerry, Ranking Member; Inouye; Breaux
Majority Professional Staff Member: Clark LeBlanc,
224-8172, SH-428
Minority Senior Staff Member: Penny Dalton, 224-4912,
SD-566

Science, Technology, and Space
224-8172, SH-428
Republicans: Frist, Chair; Burns; Hutchinson; Stevens;
Abraham
Democrats: Breaux, Ranking Member; Rockefeller; Kerry;
Dorgan
Majority Counsel: Lloyd Deschamp, 224-8172, SH-428
Minority Senior Staff Member: Penny Dalton, 224-0411,
SD-558

Surface Transportation and Merchant Marine
224-4852, SH-427
Republicans: Hutchinson, Chair; Stevens, Burns; Snowe;
Frist; Abraham, Ashcroft; Brownback
Democrats: Inouye, Ranking Member; Breaux; Dorgan;
Bryan; Wyden; Cleland
Majority Professional Staff Members: Ann Begeman,
Charlotte Casey, 224-4852, SH-427
Minority Senior Counsel: Carl Bentzel, 224-0411, SD-558

SENATE ENERGY AND NATURAL RESOURCES COMMITTEE
Phone: 224-4971
Room: SD-364

Republicans
Frank H. Murkowski (AK), Chair
Pete V. Domenici (NM)
Don Nickles (OK)
Larry E. Craig (ID)
Ben Nighthorse Campbell (CO)
Craig Thomas (WY)
Gordon Smith (OR)
Jim Bunning (KY)
Peter G. Fitzgerald (IL)
Slade Gorton (WA)
Conrad Burns (MT)

Majority Staff Director
Andrew Lundquist
224-4971, SD-364

Democrats
Jeff Bingaman (NM), Ranking Member
Daniel K. Akaka (HI)
Byron L. Dorgan (ND)
Bob Graham (FL)
Ron Wyden (OR)
Tim Johnson (SD)
Mary Landrieu (LA)
Evan Bayh (IN)
Blanche L. Lincoln (AR)

Minority Staff Director
Bob Simon
224-4103, SD-312

Senate Energy and Natural Resources Subcommittees

Energy Research, Development, Production, and Regulation
224-8115, SD-308
Republicans: Nickles, Chair; Domenici; Bunning; Gorton;
Craig; Fitzgerald; Smith
Democrats: Graham, Ranking Member; Akaka; Dorgan;
Johnson; Landrieu; Bayh
Majority Counsel: Colleen Deegan, 224-7933, SD-308
Minority Chief Counsel: Sam Fowler, 224-4103, SD-312

Forests and Public Land Management
224-6170, SD-306
Republicans: Craig, Chair; Burns; Fitzgerald; Campbell;
Domenici; Thomas; Smith
Democrats: Wyden, Ranking Member; Graham; Landrieu;
Bayh; Lincoln
Majority Professional Staff Member: Mark Rey, 224-6170,
SD-306
Minority Counsel: Kira Finkler, 224-4103, SD-312

Parks, Historic Preservation, and Recreation
224-6969, SD-354
Republicans: Thomas, Chair: Campbell; Burns; Nickles;
Bunning; Gorton
Democrats: Akaka, Ranking Member; Graham; Landrieu;
Bayh; Lincoln
Majority Professional Staff Member: Jim O'Toole, 224-6969,
SD-354
Minority Senior Counsel: David Brooks, 224-4103, SD-312

Water and Power
224-2564, SH-312
Republicans: Smith, Chair; Gorton; Bunning; Craig;
Campbell
Democrats: Dorgan, Ranking Member; Graham; Wyden;
Lincoln
Majority Counsel: Colleen Deegan, 224-2564, SH-312
Minority Senior Counsel: David Brooks, 224-4103, SD-312

SENATE ENVIRONMENT AND PUBLIC WORKS COMMITTEE
Phone: 224-6176
Room: SD-410

Republicans
John H. Chafee (RI), Chair
John W. Warner (VA)
Robert C. Smith (NH)
James M. Inhofe (OK)
Craig Thomas (WY)
Christopher S. Bond (MO)
George V. Voinovich (OH)
Michael D. Crapo (ID)
Robert Bennett (UT)
Kay Bailey Hutchison (TX)

Democrats
Max Baucus (MT), Ranking Member
Daniel Patrick Moynihan (NY)
Frank R. Lautenberg (NJ)
Harry Reid (NV)
Bob Graham (FL)
Joseph I. Lieberman (CT)
Barbara Boxer (CA)
Ron Wyden (OR)

Majority Staff Director
Jimmie Powell
224-6176, SD-410

Minority Staff Director
Tom Sliter
224-8832, SD-456

Senate Environment and Public Works Subcommittees

Clean Air, Wetlands, Private Property, and Nuclear Safety
224-6176, SD-410
Republicans: Inhofe, Chair; Voinovich; Bennett; Hutchison
Democrats: Graham, Ranking Member; Lieberman; Boxer
Majority Staff Director: Jimmie Powell, 224-2376, SD-410
Minority Professional Staff Member: Chris Miller, 224-8832,
SD-456

Fisheries, Wildlife, and Drinking Water
224-6176, SD-410
Republicans: Crapo, Chair; Thomas; Bond; Warner; Bennett;
Hutchison
Democratic: Reid, Ranking Member; Lautenberg; Wyden;
Graham; Boxer
Majority Staff Director: Jimmie Powell, 224-6176, SD-410
Minority Professional Staff Member: Jo Ellen Darcy, 224-
3247, SH-508

Superfund, Waste Control, and Risk Assessment
224-6176, SD-410
Republicans: Smith, Chair; Warner; Inhofe; Crapo
Democrats: Lautenberg, Ranking Member; Moynihan; **Boxer**
Majority Deputy Staff Director: Tom Gibson, 224-5761, **SH-**
415
Minority Professional Staff Member: Barbara Rogers, 224-
9097, SH-508

Transportation and Infrastructure
224-6176, SD-410
Republicans: Voinovich, Chair; Warner; Smith; Bond;
Inhofe; Thomas
Democrats: Baucus, Ranking Member; Moynihan; Reid;
Graham; Lieberman
Majority Professional Staff Member: Dan Corbett, 224-6176,
SD-410
Minority Professional Staff Member: Tom Sliter, 224-3333,
SH-508

SENATE FINANCE COMMITTEE
Phone: 224-4515
Room: SD-219

Republicans
William V. Roth, Jr., (DE), Chair
John H. Chafee (RI)
Charles E. Grassley (IA)
Orrin G. Hatch (UT)
Frank H. Murkowski (AK)
Don Nickles (OK)
Phil Gramm (TX)
Trent Lott (MS)
Jim M. Jeffords (VT)
Connie Mack (FL)
Fred Thompson (TN)

Majority Staff Director
Frank Polk
224-4515, SD-219

Democrats
Daniel Patrick Moynihan (NY), Ranking Member
Max Baucus (MT)
John D. Rockefeller IV (WV)
John B. Breaux (LA)
Kent Conrad (ND)
Bob Graham (FL)
Richard H. Bryan (NV)
J. Robert Kerrey (NE)
Charles Robb (VA)

Minority Staff Director
Mark Patterson
224-5315, SH-203

Senate Finance Subcommittees

Health Care
224-4515, SD-219
Republicans: Chafee, Chair; Roth; Jeffords; Grassley;
    Gramm; Nickles; Hatch; Thompson
Democrats: Rockefeller, Ranking Member; Baucus; Breaux;
    Conrad; Graham; Bryan; Kerrey
Majority Staff Director: Frank Polk, 244-4515, SD-219
Minority Staff Director: Mark Patterson, 224-5315, SH-203

International Trade
224-4515, SD-219
Republicans: Grassley, Chair; Thompson; Murkowski; Roth;
    Lott; Gramm; Hatch; Chafee; Jeffords
Democrats: Moynihan, Ranking Member; Baucus;
    Rockefeller; Breaux; Conrad; Graham; Kerrey; Robb
Majority Staff Director: Frank Polk, 224-4515, SD-219
Minority Staff Director: Mark Peterson, 224-5315, SH-203

Long-Term Growth and Debt Reduction
224-4515, SD-219
Republicans: Murkowski, Chair; Mack; Chafee

Democrats: Graham, Ranking Member; Bryan
Majority Staff Director: Frank Polk, 224-4515, SD-219
Minority Staff Director: Mark Patterson, 224-5315, SH-203

Social Security and Family Policy
224-4515, SD-219
Republicans: Nickles, Chair; Gramm; Lott; Jeffords; Chafee;
    Thompson
Democrats: Breaux, Ranking Member; Moynihan,
    Rockefeller; Kerry; Robb
Majority Staff Director: Lindy Paull, 224-4515, SD-219
Minority Staff Director: Mark Patterson, 224-5315, SH-203

Taxation and IRS Oversight
224-4515, SD-219
Republicans: Hatch, Chair; Lott; Nickles; Mack;
    Murkowski; Grassley; Thompson
Democrats: Baucus, Ranking Member; Moynihan; Conrad;
    Bryan; Robb
Majority Staff Director: Frank Polk, 224-4515, SD-219
Minority Staff Director: Mark Patterson, 224-5315, SH-203

SENATE HEALTH, EDUCATION, LABOR, AND PENSIONS COMMITTEE
Phone: 224-5375
Room: SD-428

Republicans
Jim Jeffords (VT), Chair
Judd Gregg (NH)
Bill Frist (TN)
Mike DeWine (OH)
Michael Enzi (WY)
Tim Hutchinson (AR)
Susan Collins (ME)
Chuck Hagel (NE)
Jeff Sessions (AL)
Sam Brownback (KS)

Majority Staff Director
Mark Powden
224-6770, SH-835

Democrats
Edward Kennedy (MA), Ranking Member
Christopher Dodd
Tom Harkin (IA)
Barbara Mikulski (MD)
Jeff Bingaman (NM)
Paul Wellstone (MN)
Patty Murray (WA)
Jack Reed (RI)

Minority Staff Director
Michael Myers
224-0767, SD-644

Senate Health, Education, Labor, and Pensions Subcommittees

Aging
224-0136, SH-615
Republicans: DeWine, Chair; Jeffords; Hutchinson; Gregg
Democrats: Mikulski, Ranking Member; Murray; Dodd
Majority Staff Director: Kimberly Spalding, 224-0136, SH-615
Minority Staff Director: Lynne Lawrence, 224-7962, SH-113

Children and Families
224-5800, SH-625
Republicans: Gregg, Chair; Frist; DeWine; Collins; Brownback; Hagel
Democrats: Dodd, Ranking Member; Bingaman; Wellstone; Murray; Reed
Majority Staff Director: Stephanie Monroe, 224-6211, SH-625
Minority Staff Director: Suzanne Day, 224-5630, SH-404

Employment, Safety, and Training
224-2962, SH-608
Republicans: Enzi, Chair; Jeffords; Hutchinson; Hagel; Sessions
Democrats: Wellstone, Ranking Member; Kennedy; Dodd; Harkin
Majority Staff Member: Saira Sultan, 224-2962, SH-206
Minority Staff Director: Bobby Silverstein, 224-0767, SD-646

Public Health
224-7139, SD-422
Republicans: Frist, Chair; Gregg; Enzi; Collins; Brownback; Sessions
Democrats: Kennedy, Ranking Member; Harkin; Mikulski; Bingaman; Reed
Majority Staff Director: Sue Ramthum, 224-7139, SD-422
Minority Staff Director: David Nexon, 224-7675, SH-113

SENATE INDIAN AFFAIRS COMMITTEE
Phone: 224-2251
Room: SH-838

Republicans
Ben Nighthorse Campbell (CO), Chair
Frank H. Murkowski (AK)
John McCain (AZ)
Slade Gorton (WA)
Pete V. Domenici (NM)
Craig Thomas (WY)
Orrin G. Hatch (UT)
James M. Inhofe (OK)

Majority Staff Director
Paul Moorehead
224-2251, SH-838

no subcommittees

Democrats
Daniel K. Inouye (HI), Ranking Member
Kent Conrad (ND)
Harry Reid (NV)
Daniel K. Akaka (HI)
Paul David Wellstone (MN)
Byron L. Dorgan (ND)

Minority Staff Director
Patricia Zell
224-2251, SH-838

SENATE JUDICIARY COMMITTEE
Phone: 224-5225
Room: SD-224

Republicans
Orrin G. Hatch (UT), Chair
Strom Thurmond (SC)
Charles E. Grassley (IA)
Arlen Specter (PA)
Jon L. Kyl (AZ)
Mike DeWine (OH)
John Ashcroft (MO)
Spencer Abraham (MI)
Jeff Sessions (AL)
Robert Smith (NH)

Majority Staff Director
Manus Cooney
224-5225, SD-224

Democrats
Patrick J. Leahy (VT), Ranking Member
Edward M. Kennedy (MA)
Joseph R. Biden, Jr. (DE)
Herbert H. Kohl (WI)
Dianne Feinstein (CA)
Russ Feingold (WI)
Robert G. Torricelli (NJ)
Charles Schumer (NY)

Minority Staff Director/Chief Counsel
Bruce Cohen
224-7703, SD-152

Senate Judiciary Subcommittees

Administrative Oversight and the Courts
224-6736, SH-308
Republicans: Grassley, Chair; Sessions; Thurmond; Abraham
Democrats: Toricelli, Ranking Member; Feingold; Schumer
Majority Chief Counsel: Kolan Davis, 224-6736, SH-308
Minority Chief Counsels: Matt Tanielan, Jennifer Leach, 224-4022, SD-153

Antitrust, Business Rights, and Competition
224-9494, SD-161
Republicans: DeWine, Chair; Hatch; Specter; Thurmond
Democrats: Kohl, Ranking Member; Toricelli; Leahy
Majority Chief Counsel: Louis Dupart, 224-9494, SD-161
Minority Chief Counsel: Jon Leibowitz, 224-3406, SH-815

Constitution, Federalism, and Property Rights
224-8081, SD-524
Republicans: Ashcroft, Chair; Hatch; Smith; Specter; Thurmond
Democrats: Feingold, Ranking Member; Kennedy; Leahy
Majority Counsel: Paul Clement, 224-8081, SD-524
Minority Counsel: Bob Schiff, 224-5573, SH-807

Criminal Justice Oversight
224-5225, SD-224
Republicans: Thurmond, Chair; DeWine; Ashcroft; Abraham; Sessions

Democrats: Schumer, Ranking Member; Biden; Toricelli; Leahy
Majority Chief Counsel: Garry Malphrus, 224-5225, SD-224
Minority Chief Counsel: Vacancy, 224-7703, SD-152

Immigration
224-6098, SD-323
Republicans: Abraham, Chair; Specter; Grassley; Kyl
Democrats: Kennedy, Ranking Member; Feinstein; Schumer
Majority Chief Counsel: Lee Otis, 224-6098, SD-323
Minority Chief Counsel: Melanie Barnes, 224-7878, SD-520

Technology, Terrorism, and Government Information
224-6791, SH-325
Republicans: Kyl, Chair; Hatch; Grassley; DeWine
Democrats: Feinstein, Ranking Member; Biden; Kohl
Majority Chief Counsel: Stephen Higgins, 224-4521, SH-702
Minority Chief Counsel: Neil Quinter, 224-4933, SH-807

Youth Violence
224-7572, SD-518
Republicans: Sessions, Chair; Smith; Kyl; Ashcroft
Democrats: Biden, Ranking Member; Feinstein; Kohl
Majority Chief Counsel: Kristi Lee, 224-2808, SD-163
Minority Staff Director: Chris Putala, 224-7703, SD-148

SENATE VETERANS' AFFAIRS COMMITTEE
Phone: 224-9126
Room: SR-412

Republicans
Arlen Specter (PA), Chair
Strom Thurmond (SC)
Frank Murkowski (AK)
Jim M. Jeffords (VT)
Ben Nighthorse Campbell (CO)
Larry E. Craig (ID)
Tim Hutchinson (AR)

Majority Staff Director
Charles Battaglia
224-9126, SR-412

Majority General Counsel
Bill Turek
224-9126, SR-412

no subcommittees

Democrats
John D. Rockefeller IV (WV), Ranking Member
Bob Graham (FL)
Daniel K. Akaka (HI)
Paul David Wellstone (MN)
Patty Murray (WA)

Minority Staff Director/Chief Counsel
Jim Gottlieb
224-2074, SH-202

SENATE SPECIAL COMMITTEE ON AGING
Phone: 224-5364
Room: SD-G31

Republicans
Charles E. Grassley (IA), Chair
Jim M. Jeffords (VT)
Larry E. Craig (ID)
Conrad Burns (MT)
Richard C. Shelby (AL)
Rick Santorum (PA)
Chuck Hagel (NE)
Susan M. Collins (ME)

Democrats
John B. Breaux (LA), Ranking Member
Harry Reid (NV)
Herbert H. Kohl (WI)
Russ Feingold (WI)
Ron Wyden (OR)
Jack Reed (RI)
Richard Bryan (NV)
Evan Bayh (IN)

Michael B. Enzi (WY)
Tim Hutchinson (AR)
Jim Bunning (KY)

Majority Staff Director
Ted Totman
224-5364, SD-G31

no subcommittees

Blanche Lincoln (AR)

Minority Staff Director
Ken Cohen
224-1467, SH-628

House of Representatives Leadership

Area code is 202 for all numbers.
Speaker
J. Dennis Hastert (R-14th IL)
Chief of Staff: Scott Palmer
Office: H-232
Phone: 225-0600

Majority Leader
Richard Armey (R-26th TX)
Chief of Staff: David Hobbs
Office: H-327A
Phone: 225-4000

Majority Whip
Tom DeLay (R-22nd TX)
Chief of Staff: Susan Hirschmann
Office: H-107
Phone: 225-0197

Republican Conference Chairman
J. C. Watts (R-4th OK)
Executive Director: Pam Pryor
Office: 1010 LHOB
Phone: 225-5107

Minority Leader
Richard Gephardt (D-3rd MO)
Chief of Staff: Steve Elmendorf
Office: H-204
Phone: 225-0100

Minority Whip
David E. Bonior (D-10th MI)
Administrative Assistant: Sarah Dufendach
Office: H-307
Phone: 225-3130

Democratic Caucus Chairman
Martin Frost (D-24th TX)
Executive Director: Matt Angle
Office: 1420 LHOB
Phone: 226-3210

Clerk of the House
Jeff Trandahl
Office: H-154
Phone: 225-7000

Chief Administrative Officer
James M. Eagen, III
Office: H-112
Phone: 225-6900

Sergeant at Arms
Wilson Livingood
Office: H-124
Phone: 225-2456

Postmaster
Steve Feller
Office: B-227 LHOB
Phone: 225-3856

Parliamentarian
Charles Johnson
Office: H-209
Phone: 225-7373

Chaplain
Rev. James David Ford
Office: HB-25
Phone: 225-2509

Representatives, Alphabetical Listing

CHOB - Cannon House Office Building—Rooms listed with 3 numbers
LHOB - Longworth House Office Building—Rooms listed with 4 numbers, beginning with 1
RHOB - Rayburn House Office Building—Rooms listed with 4 numbers, beginning with 2
FHOB - Gerald R. Ford House Office Building
OHOB - Thomas P. O'Neill, Jr., House Office Building
Area code is 202 for all numbers.

Abercrombie, Neil (D-1st HI)	1502	225-2726
Ackerman, Gary (D-5th NY)	2243	225-2601
Aderholt, Robert B. (R-4th AL)	1007	225-4876
Allen, Thomas H. (D-1st ME)	1717	225-6116
Andrews, Robert E. (D-1st NJ)	2439	225-6501
Archer, Bill (R-7th TX)	1236	225-2571
Armey, Richard K. (R-26th TX)	301	225-7772
Bachus, Spencer (R-6th AL)	442	225-4921
Baird, Brian (D-3rd WA)	1721	225-3536
Baker, Richard H. (R-6th LA)	434	225-3901
Baldacci, John E. (D-2nd ME)	1740	225-6306
Baldwin, Tammy (D-2nd WI)	1020	225-2906
Ballenger, Cass (R-10th NC)	2182	225-2576
Barcia, James (D-5th MI)	2419	225-8171
Barr, Bob (R-7th GA)	207	225-2931

Name	Room	Phone
Barrett, Bill (R-3rd NE)	2458	225-6435
Barrett, Thomas (D-5th WI)	1214	225-3571
Bartlett, Roscoe (R-6th MD)	2412	225-2721
Barton, Joe (R-6th TX)	2264	225-2002
Bass, Charles (R-2nd NH)	218	225-5206
Bateman, Herbert H. (R-1st VA)	2211	225-4261
Becerra, Xavier (D-30th CA)	1119	225-6235
Bentsen, Ken (D-25th TX)	326	225-7508
Bereuter, Doug (R-1st NE)	2184	225-4806
Berkley, Shelley (D-1st NV)	1505	225-5965
Berman, Howard L. (D-26th CA)	2330	225-4695
Berry, Marion (D-1st AR)	1113	225-4076
Biggert, July (R-13th IL)	508	225-3515
Bilbray, Brian (R-49th CA)	1530	225-2040
Bilirakis, Michael (R-9th FL)	2369	225-5755
Bishop, Sanford D., Jr. (D-2nd GA)	1433	225-3631
Blagojevich, Rod R. (D-5th IL)	331	225-4061
Bliley, Thomas J., Jr. (R-7th VA)	2409	225-2815
Blumenauer, Earl (D-3rd OR)	1406	225-4811
Blunt, Roy (R-7th MO)	217	225-6536
Boehlert, Sherwood L. (R-23rd NY)	2246	225-3665
Boehner, John A. (R-8th OH)	1011	225-6205
Bonilla, Henry (R-23rd TX)	1427	225-4511
Bonior, David E. (D-10th MI)	2207	225-2106
Bono, Mary (R-44th CA)	516	225-5330
Borski, Robert A. (D-3rd PA)	2267	225-8251
Boswell, Leonard L. (D-3rd IA)	1029	225-3806
Boucher, Rick (D-9th VA)	2329	225-3861
Boyd, F. Allen, Jr. (D-2nd FL)	107	225-5235
Brady, Kevin P. (R-8th TX)	1531	225-4901
Brady, Robert A. (D-1st PA)	216	225-4731
Brown, Corrine (D-3rd FL)	2444	225-0123
Brown, George E., Jr. (D-42nd CA)	2300	225-6161
Brown, Sherrod (D-13th OH)	201	225-3401
Bryant, Ed (R-7th TN)	408	225-2811
Burr, Richard M. (R-5th NC)	1513	225-2071
Burton, Dan (R-6th IN)	2185	225-2276
Buyer, Steve (R-5th IN)	227	225-5037
Callahan, Sonny (R-1st AL)	2466	225-4931
Calvert, Ken (R-43rd CA)	2201	225-1986
Camp, Dave (R-4th MI)	137	225-3561
Campbell, Tom (R-15th CA)	2442	225-2631
Canady, Charles (R-12th FL)	2432	225-1252
Cannon, Christopher (R-3rd UT)	118	225-7751
Capps, Lois (D-22nd CA)	1118	225-3601
Capuano, Michael E. (D-8th MA)	1232	225-5111
Cardin, Benjamin L. (D-3rd MD)	104	225-4016
Carson, Julia M. (D-10th IN)	1541	225-4011
Castle, Michael (R-At Large DE)	1227	225-4165
Chabot, Steve (R-1st OH)	129	225-2216
Chambliss, Saxby (R-8th GA)	1019	225-6531
Chenoweth, Helen (R-1st ID)	1727	225-6611
Christian-Green, Donna M. (D-Delegate VI)	1711	225-1790
Clay, William "Bill" (D-1st MO)	2306	225-2406
Clayton, Eva (D-1st NC)	2440	225-3101
Clement, Bob (D-5th TN)	2229	225-4311
Clyburn, James (D-6th SC)	319	225-3315
Coble, Howard (R-6th NC)	2468	225-3065
Coburn, Tom (R-2nd OK)	429	225-2701
Collins, Michael "Mac" (R-3rd GA)	1131	225-5901
Combest, Larry (R-19th TX)	1026	225-4005
Condit, Gary (D-18th CA)	2234	225-6131
Conyers, John, Jr. (D-14th MI)	2426	225-5126
Cook, Merrill (R-2nd UT)	1431	225-3011
Cooksey, John C. (R-5th LA)	317	225-8490
Costello, Jerry F. (D-12th IL)	2454	225-5661
Cox, Christopher (R-47th CA)	2402	225-5611
Coyne, William J. (D-14th PA)	2455	225-2301
Cramer, Robert E., Jr. (D-5th AL)	2350	225-4801
Crane, Philip M. (R-8th IL)	233	225-3711
Crowley, Joseph (D-7th NY)	1517	225-3965
Cubin, Barbara (R-At Large WY)	1114	225-2311
Cummings, Elijah (D-7th MD)	1632	225-4741
Cunningham, Randy (R-51st CA)	2238	225-5452
Danner, Pat (D-6th MO)	2262	225-7041
Davis, Danny (D-7th IL)	1222	225-5006
Davis, Jim (D-11th FL)	418	225-3376
Davis, Thomas M. III (R-11th VA)	224	225-1492
Deal, Nathan (R-9th GA)	2437	225-5211
DeFazio, Peter A. (D-4th OR)	2134	225-6416
DeGette, Diana L. (D-1st CO)	1339	225-4431
Delahunt, William (D-10th MA)	1317	225-3111
DeLauro, Rosa (D-3rd CT)	436	225-3661
DeLay, Tom (R-22nd TX)	341	225-5951
DeMint, Jim (R-4th SC)	507	225-6030
Deutsch, Peter (D-20th FL)	204	225-7931
Diaz-Balart, Lincoln (R-21st FL)	404	225-4211
Dickey, Jay (R-4th AR)	2453	225-3772
Dicks, Norman D. (D-6th WA)	2467	225-5916
Dingell, John D. (D-16th MI)	2328	225-4071
Dixon, Julian C. (D-32nd CA)	2252	225-7084
Doggett, Lloyd (D-10th TX)	328	225-4865
Dooley, Calvin (D-20th CA)	1201	225-3341
Doolittle, John (R-4th CA)	1526	225-2511
Doyle, Mike (D-18th PA)	133	225-2135
Dreier, David (R-28th CA)	237	225-2305
Duncan, John J., Jr. (R-2nd TN)	2400	225-5435
Dunn, Jennifer (R-8th WA)	432	225-7761
Edwards, Chet (D-11th TX)	2459	225-6105
Ehlers, Vernon (R-3rd MI)	1714	225-3831
Ehrlich, Robert, Jr. (R-2nd MD)	315	225-3061
Emerson, Jo Ann H. (R-8th MO)	132	225-4404
Engel, Eliot (D-17th NY)	2303	225-2464
English, Philip S. (R-21st PA)	1410	225-5406
Eshoo, Anna (D-14th CA)	205	225-8104
Etheridge, Bob (D-2nd NC)	1641	225-4531
Evans, Lane (D-17th IL)	2335	225-5905
Everett, Terry (R-2nd AL)	2312	225-2901
Ewing, Thomas (R-15th IL)	2417	225-2371
Faleomavaega, Eni F.H. (D-Delegate AS)	2422	225-8577
Farr, Sam (D-17th CA)	1221	225-2861
Fattah, Chaka (D-2nd PA)	1205	225-4001
Filner, Bob (D-50th CA)	2463	225-8045
Fletcher, Ernest L. (R-6th KY)	1117	225-4706
Foley, Mark (R-16th FL)	113	225-5792
Forbes, Michael P. (R-1st NY)	125	225-3826
Ford, Harold E., Jr. (D-9th TN)	325	225-3265
Fossella, Vito (R-13th NY)	431	225-3371
Fowler, Tillie (R-4th FL)	106	225-2501

Frank, Barney (D-4th MA)	2210	225-5931		Jackson-Lee, Sheila (D-18th TX)	410	225-3816
Franks, Bob (R-7th NJ)	225	225-5361		Jefferson, William J. (D-2nd LA)	240	225-6636
Frelinghuysen, Rodney (R-11th NJ)	228	225-5034		Jenkins, William L. (R-1st TN)	1708	225-6356
Frost, Martin (D-24th TX)	2256	225-3605		John, Chris (D-7th LA)	1504	225-2031
Gallegly, Elton (R-23rd CA)	2427	225-5811		Johnson, Eddie Bernice (D-30th TX)	1511	225-8885
Ganske, Greg (R-4th IA)	1108	225-4426		Johnson, Nancy L. (R-6th CT)	2113	225-4476
Gejdenson, Sam (D-2nd CT)	2304	225-2076		Johnson, Sam (R-3rd TX)	1030	225-4201
Gekas, George W. (R-17th PA)	2410	225-4315		Jones, Stephanie Tubbs (D-11th OH)	1516	225-7032
Gephardt, Richard A. (D-3rd MO)	1226	225-2671		Jones, Walter, Jr. (R-3rd NC)	422	225-3415
Gibbons, James A. (R-2nd NV)	100	225-6155		Kanjorski, Paul E. (D-11th PA)	2353	225-6511
Gilchrest, Wayne (R-1st MD)	2245	225-5311		Kaptur, Marcy (D-9th OH)	2366	225-4146
Gillmor, Paul E. (R-5th OH)	1203	225-6405		Kasich, John R. (R-12th OH)	1111	225-5355
Gilman, Benjamin A. (R-20th NY)	2449	225-3776		Kelly, Sue W. (R-19th NY)	1122	225-5441
Gonzalez, Charles A. (D-20th TX)	327	225-3236		Kennedy, Patrick J. (D-1st RI)	312	225-4911
Goode, Virgil H., Jr. (D-5th VA)	1520	225-4711		Kildee, Dale E. (D-9th MI)	2187	225-3611
Goodlatte, Bob (R-6th VA)	2240	225-5431		Kilpatrick, Carolyn C. (D-15th MI)	503	225-2261
Goodling, William F. (R-19th PA)	2107	225-5836		Kind, Ronald J. (D-3rd WI)	1713	225-5506
Gordon, Bart (D-6th TN)	2368	225-4231		King, Peter (R-3rd NY)	403	225-7896
Goss, Porter J. (R-14th FL)	108	225-2536		Kingston, Jack (R-1st GA)	1034	225-5831
Graham, Lindsey (R-3rd SC)	1429	225-5301		Kleczka, Jerry (D-4th WI)	2301	225-4572
Granger, Kay (R-12th TX)	435	225-5071		Klink, Ron (D-4th PA)	2448	225-2565
Green, Gene (D-29th TX)	2429	225-1688		Knollenberg, Joseph (R-11th MI)	2349	225-5802
Green, Mark (R-8th WI)	1218	225-5665		Kolbe, Jim (R-5th AZ)	2266	225-2542
Greenwood, Jim (R-8th PA)	2436	225-4276		Kucinich, Dennis J. (D-10th OH)	1730	225-5871
Gutierrez, Luis (D-4th IL)	2438	224-8203		Kuykendall, Steven T. (R-36th CA)	512	225-8220
Gutknecht, Gil (R-1st MN)	425	225-2472		LaFalce, John J. (D-29th NY)	2310	225-3231
Hall, Ralph M. (D-4th TX)	2221	225-6673		LaHood, Ray (R-18th IL)	329	225-6201
Hall, Tony P. (D-3rd OH)	1432	225-6465		Lampson, Nicholas V. (D-9th TX)	417	225-6565
Hansen, James V. (R-1st UT)	242	225-0453		Lantos, Tom (D-12th CA)	2217	225-3531
Hastert, J. Dennis (R-14th IL)	2263	225-2976		Largent, Steve (R-1st OK)	426	225-2211
Hastings, Alcee (D-23rd FL)	2235	225-1313		Larson, John B. (D-1st CT)	1419	225-2265
Hastings, Doc (R-4th WA)	1323	225-5816		Latham, Tom (R-5th IA)	324	225-5476
Hayes, Robin (R-8th NC)	130	225-3715		LaTourette, Steven C. (R-19th OH)	1224	225-5731
Hayworth, J.D. (R-6th AZ)	1023	225-2190		Lazio, Rick (R-2nd NY)	2244	225-3335
Hefley, Joel (R-5th CO)	2230	225-4422		Leach, Jim (R-1st IA)	2186	225-6576
Herger, Wally (R-2nd CA)	2433	225-3076		Lee, Barbara (D-9th CA)	414	225-2661
Hill, Baron P. (D-9th IN)	1208	225-5315		Levin, Sander M. (D-12th MI)	2268	225-4961
Hill, Rick A. (R-At Large MT)	1609	225-3211		Lewis, Jerry (R-40th CA)	2112	225-5861
Hilleary, Van (R-4th TN)	114	225-6831		Lewis, John (D-5th GA)	343	225-3801
Hilliard, Earl (D-7th AL)	1314	225-2665		Lewis, Ron (R-2nd KY)	223	225-3501
Hinchey, Maurice (D-26th NY)	2431	225-6335		Linder, John (R-11th GA)	2447	225-4272
Hinojosa, Ruben E. (D-15th TX)	1032	225-2531		Lipinski, William O. (D-3rd IL)	1501	225-5701
Hobson, David (R-7th OH)	1514	225-4324		LoBiondo, Frank A. (R-2nd NJ)	222	225-6572
Hoeffel, Joseph M., III (D-13th PA)	1229	225-6111		Lofgren, Zoe (D-16th CA)	318	225-3072
Hoekstra, Peter (R-2nd MI)	1124	225-4401		Lowey, Nita M. (D-18th NY)	2421	225-6506
Holden, Tim (D-6th PA)	1421	225-5546		Lucas, Frank D. (R-6th OK)	438	225-5565
Holt, Rush D. (D-12th NJ)	1630	225-5801		Lucas, Ken (D-4th KY)	1237	225-3465
Hooley, Darlene (D-5th OR)	1130	225-5711		Luther, Bill (D-6th MN)	117	225-2271
Horn, Steve (R-38th CA)	2331	225-6676		Maloney, Carolyn (D-14th NY)	2430	225-7944
Hostettler, John J. (R-8th IN)	1507	225-4636		Maloney, James H. (D-5th CT)	1213	225-3822
Houghton, Amo, Jr. (R-31st NY)	1110	225-3161		Manzullo, Donald (R-16th IL)	409	225-5676
Hoyer, Steny H. (D-5th MD)	1705	225-4131		Markey, Edward J. (D-7th MA)	2108	225-2836
Hulshof, Kenny C. (R-9th MO)	412	225-2956		Martinez, Matthew G. (D-31st CA)	2269	225-5464
Hunter, Duncan (R-52nd CA)	2265	225-5672		Mascara, Frank R. (D-20th PA)	314	225-4665
Hutchinson, Asa (R-3rd AR)	1535	225-4301		Matsui, Robert T. (D-5th CA)	2308	225-7163
Hyde, Henry J. (R-6th IL)	2110	225-4561		McCarthy, Carolyn (D-4th NY)	1725	225-5516
Inslee, Jay (D-6th WA)	308	225-6311		McCarthy, Karen (D-5th MO)	1330	225-4535
Isakson, Johnny (R-6th GA)	2428	225-4501		McCollum, Bill (R-8th FL)	2109	225-2176
Istook, Ernest, Jr. (R-5th OK)	2404	225-2131		McCrery, Jim (R-4th LA)	2104	225-2777
Jackson, Jesse L., Jr. (D-2nd IL)	313	225-0773		McDermott, Jim (D-7th WA)	1035	225-3106

McGovern, James P. (D-3rd MA)	416	225-6101
McHugh, John (R-24th NY)	2441	225-4611
McInnis, Scott (R-3rd CO)	320	225-4761
McIntosh, David (R-2nd IN)	1610	225-3021
McIntyre, Mike (D-7th NC)	1605	225-2731
McKeon, Howard "Buck" (R-25th CA)	2242	225-1956
McKinney, Cynthia (D-4th GA)	124	225-1605
McNulty, Michael R. (D-21st NY)	2161	225-5076
Meehan, Marty (D-5th MA)	2434	225-3411
Meek, Carrie P. (D-17th FL)	401	225-4506
Meeks, Gregory W. (D-6th NY)	1710	225-3461
Menendez, Robert (D-13th NJ)	405	225-7919
Metcalf, Jack (R-2nd WA)	1510	225-2605
Mica, John (R-7th FL)	2445	225-4035
Millender-McDonald, Juanita (D-37th CA)	419	225-7924
Miller, Dan (R-13th FL)	102	225-5015
Miller, Gary G. (R-41st CA)	1037	225-3201
Miller, George (D-7th CA)	2205	225-2095
Minge, David (D-2nd MN)	1415	225-2331
Mink, Patsy (D-2nd HI)	2135	225-4906
Moakley, Joe (D-9th MA)	235	225-8273
Mollohan, Alan B. (D-1st WV)	2346	225-4172
Moore, Dennis (D-3rd KS)	506	225-2865
Moran, James P. (D-8th VA)	2239	225-4376
Moran, Jerry (R-1st KS)	1519	225-2715
Morella, Constance A. (R-8th MD)	2228	225-5341
Murtha, John P. (D-12th PA)	2423	225-2065
Myrick, Sue (R-9th NC)	230	225-1976
Nadler, Jerrold (R-8th NY)	2334	225-5635
Napolitano, Grace F. (D-34th CA)	1407	225-5256
Neal, Richard E. (D-2nd MA)	2236	225-5601
Nethercutt, George R., Jr. (R-5th WA)	1527	225-2006
Ney, Bob (R-18th OH)	1024	225-6265
Northup, Anne M. (R-3rd KY)	1004	225-5401
Norton, Eleanor Holmes (D-Delegate DC)	1424	225-8050
Norwood, Charles (R-10th GA)	1707	225-4101
Nussle, Jim (R-2nd IA)	303	225-2911
Oberstar, James L. (D-8th MN)	2365	225-6211
Obey, David R. (D-7th WI)	2314	225-3365
Olver, John W. (D-1st MA)	1027	225-5335
Ortiz, Solomon P. (D-27th TX)	2136	225-7742
Ose, Doug (R-3rd CA)	1508	225-5716
Owens, Major R. (D-11th NY)	2305	225-6231
Oxley, Michael G. (R-4th OH)	2233	225-2676
Packard, Ron (R-48th CA)	2372	225-3906
Pallone, Frank, Jr. (D-6th NJ)	420	225-4671
Pascrell, William J., Jr. (D-8th NJ)	1722	225-5751
Pastor, Ed (D-2nd AZ)	2465	225-4065
Paul, Ron E. (R-14th TX)	203	225-2831
Payne, Donald M. (D-10th NJ)	2209	225-3436
Pease, Edward A. (R-7th IN)	119	225-5805
Pelosi, Nancy (D-8th CA)	2457	225-4965
Peterson, Collin (D-7th MN)	2159	225-2165
Peterson, John E. (R-5th PA)	307	225-5121
Petri, Thomas E. (R-6th WI)	2262	225-2476
Phelps, David D. (D-19th IL)	1523	225-5201
Pickering, Charles "Chip", Jr. (R-3rd MS)	427	225-5031
Pickett, Owen B. (D-2nd VA)	2133	225-4215
Pitts, Joseph R. (R-16th PA)	504	225-2411
Pombo, Richard (R-11th CA)	2411	225-1947
Pomeroy, Earl (D-At Large ND)	1533	225-2611
Porter, John Edward (R-10th IL)	2373	225-4835
Portman, Rob (R-2nd OH)	238	225-3164
Price, David E. (D-4th NC)	2162	225-1784
Pryce, Deborah (R-15th OH)	221	225-2015
Quinn, Jack (R-30th NY)	229	225-3306
Radanovich, George P. (R-19th CA)	123	225-4540
Rahall, Nick J., II (D-3rd WV)	2307	225-3452
Ramstad, Jim (R-3rd MN)	103	225-2871
Rangel, Charles B. (D-15th NY)	2354	225-4365
Regula, Ralph (R-16th OH)	2309	225-3876
Reyes, Silvestre (D-16th TX)	514	225-4831
Reynolds, Thomas M. (R-27th NY)	413	225-5265
Riley, Bob (R-3rd AL)	322	225-3261
Rivers, Lynn (D-13th MI)	1724	225-6261
Rodriguez, Ciro D. (D-28th TX)	323	225-1640
Roemer, Tim J. (D-3rd IN)	2352	224-3915
Rogan, James E. (R-27th CA)	126	225-4176
Rogers, Harold (R-5th KY)	2470	225-4601
Rohrabacher, Dana (R-45th CA)	2338	225-2415
Romero-Barcelo, Carlos (D-Resident Commissioner PR)	2160	225-2615
Ros-Lehtinen, Ileana (R-18th FL)	2160	225-3931
Rothman, Steve R. (D-9th NJ)	1607	225-5061
Roukema, Marge (R-5th NJ)	2469	225-4465
Roybal-Allard, Lucille (D-33rd CA)	2435	225-1766
Royce, Edward (R-39th CA)	1133	225-4111
Rush, Bobby (D-1st IL)	2416	225-4372
Ryan, Paul (R-1st WI)	1217	225-3031
Ryun, Jim R. (R-2nd KS)	330	225-6601
Sabo, Martin Olav (D-5th MN)	2336	225-4755
Salmon, Matt (R-1st AZ)	115	225-2635
Sanchez, Loretta L. (D-46th CA)	1529	225-2965
Sanders, Bernard (I-At Large VT)	2202	225-4115
Sandlin, Max A. (D-1st TX)	214	225-3035
Sanford, Mark, Jr. (R-1st SC)	1233	225-3176
Sawyer, Thomas C. (D-14th OH)	1414	225-5231
Saxton, Jim (R-3rd NJ)	339	225-4765
Scarborough, Joe (R-1st FL)	127	225-4136
Schaffer, Bob (R-4th CO)	212	225-4676
Schakowsky, Janice D. (D-9th IL)	515	225-2111
Scott, Robert "Bobby" C. (D-3rd VA)	2464	225-8351
Sensenbrenner, F. James, Jr. (R-9th WI)	2332	225-5101
Serrano, Jose (D-16th NY)	2342	225-4361
Sessions, Pete (R-5th TX)	1318	225-2231
Shadegg, John (R-4th AZ)	430	225-3361
Shaw, E. Clay, Jr. (R-22nd FL)	2408	225-3026
Shays, Christopher (R-4th CT)	1126	225-5541
Sherman, Brad (D-24th CA)	1524	225-5911
Sherwood, Don (R-10th PA)	1223	225-3731
Shimkus, John M. (R-20th IL)	513	225-5271
Shows, Ronnie (D-4th MS)	509	225-5865
Shuster, Bud (R-9th PA)	2188	225-2431
Simpson, Michael K. (R-2nd ID)	1440	225-5531
Sisisky, Norman (D-4th VA)	2371	225-6365
Skeen, Joe (R-2nd NM)	2302	225-2365
Skelton, Ike (D-4th MO)	2206	225-2876

Slaughter, Louise McIntosh (D-28th NY)	2347	225-3615	Toomey, Patrick J. (R-15th PA)	511	225-6411
Smith, Adam (D-9th WA)	116	225-8901	Towns, Edolphus (D-10th NY)	2232	225-5936
Smith, Christopher H. (R-4th NJ)	2370	225-3765	Traficant, James A., Jr. (D-17th OH)	2446	225-5261
Smith, Lamar S. (R-21st TX)	2231	225-4236	Turner, Jim (D-2nd TX)	208	225-2401
Smith, Nick (R-7th MI)	306	225-6276			
Smith, Robert F. (R-2nd OR)	1126	225-6730	Udall, Mark (D-2nd CO)	128	225-2161
Snyder, Vic (D-2nd AR)	1319	225-2506	Udall, Tom (D-3rd NM)	502	225-6190
Souder, Mark (R-4th IN)	109	225-4436	Underwood, Robert A. (D-Delegate GU)	2418	225-1188
Spence, Floyd (R-2nd SC)	2405	225-2452	Upton, Fred (R-6th MI)	2333	225-3761
Spratt, John M., Jr. (D-5th SC)	1536	225-5501			
Stabenow, Debbie (D-8th MI)	1039	225-4872	Velazquez, Nydia M. (D-12th NY)	2241	225-2361
Stark, Fortney "Pete" (D-13th CA)	239	225-5065	Vento, Bruce F. (D-4th NM)	2413	225-6631
Stearns, Cliff (R-6th FL)	2227	225-5744	Visclosky, Peter J. (D-1st IN)	2313	225-2461
Stenholm, Charles W. (D-17th TX)	1211	225-6605			
Strickland, Ted (D-6th OH)	336	225-5705	Walden, Greg (R-2nd OR)	1404	225-6730
Stump, Bob (R-3rd AZ)	211	225-4576	Walsh, James T. (R-25th NY)	2351	225-3701
Stupak, Bart (D-1st MI)	2348	225-4735	Wamp, Zach (R-3rd TN)	423	225-3271
Sununu, John E. (R-1st NH)	316	225-5456	Waters, Maxine (D-35th CA)	2344	225-2201
Sweeney, John E. (R-22nd NY)	437	225-5614	Watkins, Wes (R-3rd OK)	1401	225-4565
			Watt, Melvin L. (D-12th NC)	1230	225-1510
Talent, James (R-2nd MO)	1022	225-2561	Watts, J.C., Jr. (R-4th OK)	1210	225-6165
Tancredo, Thomas G. (R-6th CO)	1123	225-7882	Waxman, Henry A. (D-29th CA)	2204	225-3976
Tanner, John S. (D-8th TN)	1127	225-4714	Weiner, Anthony D. (D-9th NY)	501	225-6616
Tauscher, Ellen O. (D-10th CA)	1239	225-1880	Weldon, Curt (R-7th PA)	2452	225-2011
Tauzin, W.J. "Billy" (R-3rd LA)	2183	225-4031	Weldon, Dave (R-15th FL)	332	225-3671
Taylor, Charles H. (R-11th NC)	231	225-6401	Weller, Jerry (R-11th IL)	424	225-3635
Taylor, Gene (D-5th MS)	2311	225-5772	Wexler, Robert (D-19th FL)	213	225-3001
Terry, Lee (R-2nd NE)	1728	225-4155	Weygand, Robert A. (D-2nd RI)	215	225-2735
Thomas, William M. (R-21st CA)	2208	225-2915	Whitfield, Ed (R-1st KY)	236	225-3115
Thompson, Bennie G. (D-2nd MS)	1408	225-5876	Wicker, Roger F. (R-1st MS)	206	225-4306
Thompson, Mike (D-1st CA)	415	225-3311	Wilson, Heather (R-1st NM)	226	225-6316
Thornberry, William "Mac" (R-13th TX)	131	225-3706	Wise, Robert E., Jr. (D-2nd WV)	2367	225-2711
			Wolf, Frank R. (R-10th VA)	241	225-5136
Thune, John R. (R-At Large SD)	1005	225-2801	Woolsey, Lynn (D-6th CA)	439	225-5161
Thurman, Karen L. (D-5th FL)	440	225-1002	Wu, David (D-1st OR)	510	225-0855
Tiahrt, Todd (R-4th KS)	428	225-6216	Wynn, Albert Russell (D-4th MD)	407	225-8699
Tierney, John F. (D-6th MA)	120	225-8020	Young, C.W. Bill (R-10th FL)	2407	225-5961
			Young, Don (R-At Large AK)	2111	225-5765

Key House Committees

Area code is 202 for all numbers.

HOUSE APPROPRIATIONS COMMITTEE
Phone: 225-2771
Room: H-218 Capitol
http://www.house.gov.appropriations

Republicans	**Democrats**
C.W. Bill Young (FL), Chair	David R. Obey (WI), Ranking Member
Ralph Regula (OH)	John P. Murtha (PA)
Jerry Lewis (CA)	Norman D. Dicks (WA)
John Edward Porter (IL)	Martin Olav Sabo (MN)
Harold Rogers (KY)	Julian C. Dixon (CA)
Joe Skeen (NM)	Steny H. Hoyer (MD)
Frank R. Wolf (VA)	Alan B. Mollohan (WV)
Tom DeLay (TX)	Marcy Kaptur (OH)
Jim Kolbe (AZ)	Nancy Pelosi (CA)
Ron Packard (CA)	Peter J. Visclosky (IN)
Sonny Callahan (AL)	Nita M. Lowey (NY)
James T. Walsh (NY)	Jose Serrano (NY)
Charles H. Taylor (NC)	Rosa DeLauro (CT)

David Hobson (OH)
Ernest Istook, Jr. (OK)
Henry Bonilla (TX)
Joseph Knollenberg (MI)
Dan Miller (FL)
Jay Dickey (AR)
Jack Kingston (GA)
Rodney Frelinghuysen (NJ)
Roger Wicker (MS)
Michael P. Forbes (NY)
George R. Nethercutt, Jr. (WA)
Randy Cunningham (CA)
Todd Tiahrt (KS)
Zach Wamp (TN)
Tom Latham (IA)
Anne M. Northup (KY)
Robert B. Aderholt (AL)
Jo Ann Emerson (MS)
John E. Sununu (NH)
Kay Granger (TX)
John E. Peterson (PA)

Majority Staff Director
James E. Dyer
225-2771, H-218 Capitol

House Appropriations Subcommittees

Agriculture, Rural Development, Food and Drug Administration, and Related Agencies
225-2638, 2362A RHOB
Republicans: Skeen, Chair; Walsh; Dickey; Kingston; Nethercutt; Bonilla; Latham; Emerson
Democrats: Kaptur, Ranking Member; DeLauro; Hinchey; Farr; Boyd
Majority Professional Staff Member: Hank Moore, 225-2638, 2362A RHOB
Minority Professional Staff Member: Sally Chadbourne, 225-3481, 1016 LHOB

Commerce, Justice, State, and the Judiciary
225-3351, H-309 Capitol
Republicans: Rogers, Chair; Kolbe; Taylor; Regula; Latham; Miller; Wamp
Democrats: Serrano, Ranking Member; Dixon; Mollohan; Roybal-Allard
Majority Professional Staff Member: Jim Kulikowski, 225-3351, H-309 Capitol
Minority Professional Staff Members: Patricia Schlueter, David Reich, 225-3481, 1016 LHOB

Defense
225-2847, H-149 Capitol
Republicans: Lewis, Chair; Young; Skeen; Hobson; Bonilla; Nethercutt; Istook; Cunningham; Dickey; Frelinghuysen
Democrats: Murtha, Ranking Member; Dicks; Sabo; Dixon; Visclosky; Moran
Majority Professional Staff Member: Kevin Roper, 225-2847, H-149 Capitol
Minority Professional Staff Member: Greg Dahlberg, 225-3481, 1016 LHOB

James P. Moran (VA)
John W. Olver (MA)
Ed Pastor (AZ)
Carrie Meek (FL)
David E. Price (NC)
Chet Edwards (TX)
Robert E. "Bud" Cramer, Jr. (AL)
James E. Clyburn (SC)
Maurice D. Hinchey (NY)
Lucille Roybal-Allard (CA)
Sam Farr (CA)
Jesse L. Jackson, Jr. (IL)
Carolyn C. Kilpatrick (MI)
Allen Boyd (FL)

Minority Staff Director
Scott Lilly
225-3481, 1016 LHOB

District of Columbia
225-5338, H-147 Capitol
Republicans: Istook, Chair; Cunningham; Tiahrt; Aderholt; Emerson; Sununu
Democrats: Moran, Ranking Member; Dixon; Mollohan
Majority Professional Staff Member: Americo Miconi, 225-5338, H-147 Capitol
Minority Professional Staff Member: Cheryl Smith, 225-3481, 1016 LHOB

Energy and Water Development
225-3421, 2362B RHOB
Republicans: Packard, Chair; Rogers; Knollenberg; Forbes; Frelinghuysen; Callahan; Latham
Democrats: Visclosky, Ranking Member; Edwards; Pastor; Clyburn
Majority Professional Staff Member: Jim Ogsbury, 225-3421, 2362B RHOB
Minority Professional Staff Member: Sally Chadbourne, 225-3481, 1016 LHOB

Foreign Operations, Export Financing, and Related Programs
225-2041, H-150 Capitol
Republicans: Callahan, Chair; Porter; Wolf; Packard; Knollenberg; Forbes; Kingston; Lewis
Democrats: Pelosi, Ranking Member; Lowey; Jackson; Kilpatrick; Sabo
Majority Professional Staff Member: Charlie Flickner, 225-2041, H-150 Capitol
Minority Professional Staff Member: Mark Murray, 225-3481, 1016 LHOB

Interior
225-3081, B-308 RHOB
Republicans: Regula, Chair; Kolbe; Skeen; Taylor; Nethercutt; Wamp; Kingston; Peterson

Democrats: Dicks, Ranking Member; Murtha; Moran;
Cramer; Hinchey
Majority Professional Staff Member: Debbie Weatherly,
225-3081, B-308 RHOB
Minority Professional Staff Member: Del Davis, 225-3481,
1016 LHOB

Labor, Health and Human Services, and Education
225-3508, 2358 RHOB
Republicans: Porter, Chair; Young; Bonilla; Istook; Miller;
Dickey; Wicker; Northup; Cunningham
Democrats: Obey, Ranking Member; Hoyer; Pelosi; Lowey;
DeLauro; Jackson
Majority Professional Staff Member: Tony McCann,
225-3508, 2358 RHOB
Minority Professional Staff Members: Mark Mioduski,
Cheryl Smith, 225-3481, 1016 LHOB

Legislative
225-5338, H-147 Capitol
Republicans: Taylor, Chair; Wamp; Lewis; Granger; Peterson
Democrats: Pastor, Ranking Member; Murtha; Hoyer
Majority Professional Staff Member: Ed Lombard, 225-5338,
H-147 Capitol
Minority Professional Staff Member: Greg Dahlberg,
225-3481, 1016 LHOB

Military Construction
225-3047, B-300 RHOB
Republicans: Hobson, Chair; Porter; Wicker; Tiahrt; Walsh;
Miller; Aderholt; Granger
Democrats: Olver, Ranking Member; Edwards; Farr; Boyd;
Dicks

Majority Professional Staff Member: Liz Dawson, 225-3047,
B-300 RHOB
Minority Professional Staff Member: Mark Murray,
225-3481, 1016 LHOB

Transportation
225-2141, 2358 RHOB
Republicans: Wolf, Chair; DeLay; Regula; Rogers; Packard;
Callahan; Tiahrt; Aderholt; Granger
Democrats: Sabo, Ranking Member; Olver; Pastor;
Kilpatrick; Serrano; Clyburn
Majority Professional Staff Member: John Blazey, 225-2141,
2358 RHOB
Minority Professional Staff Member: Cheryl Smith,
225-3481, 1016 LHOB

Treasury, Postal Service, and General Government
225-5834, B-307 RHOB
Republicans: Kolbe, Chair; Wolf; Forbes; Northup; Emerson;
Sununu; Peterson
Democrats: Hoyer, Ranking Member; Meek; Price;
Roybal-Allard
Majority Professional Staff Member: Patricia Schlueter,
225-3481, 1016 LHOB

VA, HUD, and Independent Agencies
225-3241, H-143 Capitol
Republicans: Walsh, Chair; DeLay; Hobson; Knollenberg;
Frelinghuysen; Wicker; Northrup; Sununu
Democrats: Mollohan, Ranking Member; Kaptur; Meek;
Price; Cramer
Majority Staff Director: Frank Cushing, 225-3241, H-143
Capitol
Minority Professional Staff Members: Del Davis, David
Reich, 225-3481, 1016 LHOB

HOUSE BUDGET COMMITTEE
Phone: 226-7270
Room: 309 CHOB
http://www.house.gov/budget/

Republicans
John R. Kasich (OH), Chair
Saxby Chambliss (GA)
Christopher Shays (CT)
Wally Herger (CA)
Bob Franks (NJ)
Nick Smith (MI)
Jim Nussle (IA)
Peter Hoekstra (MI)
George P. Radanovich (CA)
Charles F. Bass (NH)
Gil Gutknecht (MN)
Van Hilleary (TN)
John E. Sununu (NH)
Joseph R. Pitts (PA)
Joe Knollenberg (MI)
William "Mac" Thornberry (TX)
Jim Ryun (KS)
Mac Collins (GA)
Zach Wamp (TN)
Mark Green (WI)
Ernie Fletcher (KY)
Gary Miller (CA)
Paul Ryan (WI)
Pat Toomey (PA)

Democrats
John M. Spratt, Jr. (SC), Ranking Member
Jim McDermott (WA)
Lynn Rivers (MI)
Bennie G. Thompson (MS)
David Minge (MN)
Ken Bentsen (TX)
Jim Davis (FL)
Bob Weygand (RI)
Eva Clayton (NC)
David Price (NC)
Ed Markey (MA)
Jerry Kleczka (WI)
Bob Clement (TN)
Jim Moran (VA)
Darlene Hooley (OR)
Ken Lucas (KY)
Rush Holt (NJ)
Joseph Hoeffel (PA)
Tammy Baldwin (WI)

Majority Staff Director
Wayne T. Struble
226-7270, 309 CHOB

no subcommittees

Minority Staff Director/Chief Counsel
Thomas S. Kahn
226-7200, 222 OHOB

HOUSE COMMERCE COMMITTEE
Phone: 225-2927
Room: 2125 RHOB
http://www.house.gov/commerce

Republicans
Thomas J. Bliley, Jr. (VA), Chair
W.J. "Billy" Tauzin (LA)
Michael G. Oxley (OH)
Michael Bilirakis (FL)
Joe Barton (TX)
Fred Upton (MI)
Cliff Stearns (FL)
Paul E. Gillmor (OH)
James C. Greenwood (PA)
Christopher Cox (CA)
Nathan Deal (GA)
Steve Largent (OK)
Richard M. Burr (NC)
Brian P. Bilbray (CA)
Ed Whitfield (KY)
Greg Ganske (IA)
Charlie Norwood (GA)
Tom Coburn (OK)
Rick Lazio (NY)
Barbara Cubin (WY)
James E. Rogan (CA)
John M. Shimkus (IL)
Heather Wilson (NM)
John B. Shadegg (AZ)
Charles W. "Chip" Pickering Jr. (MS)
Vito Fossella (NY)
Roy Blunt (MS)
Ed Bryant (TN)
Robert L. Erlich, Jr. (MD)

Majority Staff Director
James Derderian
225-2927, 2125 RHOB

Democrats
John D. Dingell (MI), Ranking Member
Henry A. Waxman (CA)
Edward J. Markey (MA)
Ralph M. Hall (TX)
Rick Boucher (VA)
Edolphus Towns (NY)
Frank Pallone, Jr. (NJ)
Sherrod Brown (OH)
Bart Gordon (TN)
Peter Deutsch (FL)
Bobby Rush (IL)
Anna Eshoo (CA)
Ron Klink (PA)
Bart Stupak (MI)
Eliot Engel (NY)
Thomas C. Sawyer (OH)
Albert Wynn (MD)
Gene Green (TX)
Karen McCarthy (MO)
Ted Strickland (OH)
Diana L. DeGette (CO)
Thomas M. Barrett (WI)
Bill Luther (MN)
Lois Capps (CA)

Minority Staff Director
Reid Stuntz
225-3641, 2322 RHOB

House Commerce Subcommittees

Energy and Power
225-2927, 2125 RHOB
Republicans: Barton, Chair; Bilirakis; Stearns; Largent; Burr; Whitfield; Norwood; Coburn; Rogan; Shimkus; Wilson; Shadegg; Pickering; Fossella; Bryant; Erlich; Bliley (ex officio)
Democrats: Hall, Ranking Member; McCarthy; Sawyer; Markey; Boucher; Pallone; Brown; Gordon; Rush; Wynn; Strickland; Deutsch; Klink; Dingell (ex officio)
Majority Staff Director: James Derderian, 225-2927, 2125 RHOB
Minority Staff Director: Reid Stuntz, 225-3641, 2322 RHOB

Finance and Hazardous Materials
225-2927, 2125 RHOB
Republicans: Oxley, Chair; Tauzin; Gillmor; Greenwood;

Cox; Largent; Bilbray; Ganske; Lazio; Shimkus; Wilson; Shadegg; Fossella; Blunt; Erlich; Bliley (ex officio)
Democrats: Towns, Ranking Member; Deutsch; Stupak; Engel; DeGette; Barrett; Luther; Capps; Markey; Hall; Pallone; Rush; Dingell (ex officio)
Majority Staff Director: James Derderian, 225-2927, 2125 RHOB
Minority Staff Director: Reid Stuntz, 225-3641, 2322 RHOB

Health and Environment
225-2927, 2125 RHOB
Republicans: Bilirakis, Chair; Upton; Stearns; Greenwood; Deal; Burr; Bilbray; Whitfield; Ganske; Norwood; Coburn; Lazio; Cubin; Shadegg; Pickering; Bryant
Democrats: Brown, Ranking Member; Waxman; Pallone; Deutsch; Stupak; Green; Strickland; DeGette; Barrett; Capps; Hall; Towns; Eshoo
Majority Staff Director: James Derderian, 225-2927, 2125 RHOB
Minority Staff Director: Reid Stuntz, 225-3641, 2322 RHOB

Oversight and Investigations
225-2927, 2125 RHOB
Republicans: Upton, Chair; Barton; Cox; Burr; Bilbray; Whitfield; Ganske; Blunt; Bryant

Democrats: Klink, Ranking Member; Waxman; Stupak; Green; McCarthy; Strickland; DeGette
Majority Staff Director: James Derderian, 225-2927, 2125 RHOB
Minority Staff Director: Reid Stuntz, 225-3641, 2322 RHOB

Telecommunications, Trade, and Consumer Protection
225-2927, 2125 RHOB
Republicans: Tauzin, Chair; Oxley; Stearns; Gillmor; Cox; Deal; Largent; Cubin; Rogan; Shimkus; Wilson; Pickering; Fossella; Blunt; Ehrlich
Democrats: Markey, Ranking Member; Boucher; Gordon; Rush; Eshoo; Engel; Wynn; Luther; Klink; Sawyer; Green; McCarthy
Majority Staff Director: James Derderian, 225-2927, 2125 RHOB
Minority Staff Director: Reid Stuntz, 225-3641, 2322 RHOB

HOUSE EDUCATION AND WORKFORCE COMMITTEE
Phone: 225-4527
Room: 2181 RHOB
http://www.house.gov/eeo

Republicans
William (Bill) Goodling (PA), Chair
Thomas E. Petri (WI)
Marge Roukema (NJ)
Cass Ballenger (NC)
Bill Barrett (NE)
John A. Boehner (OH)
Peter Hoekstra (MI)
Howard P. "Buck" McKeon (CA)
Michael N. Castle (DE)
Sam Johnson (TX)
James M. Talent (MO)
James C. Greenwood (PA)
Lindsey O. Graham (SC)
Mark E. Souder (IN)
David M. McIntosh (IN)
Charlie Norwood (GA)
Ron Paul (TX)
Bob Schaffer (CO)
Fred Upton (MI)
Nathan Deal (GA)
Van Hilleary (TN)
Venon J. Ehlers (MI)
Matt Salmon (AZ)
Tom Tancredo (CO)
Ernie Fletcher (KY)
Jim DeMint (SC)
Johnny Isakson (GA)

Majority Staff Director
Kevin Talley
225-4527, 2181 RHOB

Democrats
William (Bill) Clay (MO), Ranking Member
George Miller (CA)
Dale E. Kildee (MI)
Matthew G. Martinez (CA)
Major R. Owens (NY)
Donald M. Payne (NJ)
Patsy T. Mink (HI)
Robert E. Andrews (NJ)
Timothy J. Roemer (IN)
Robert C. (Bobby) Scott (VA)
Lynn C. Woolsey (CA)
Carlos A. Romero-Barcelo (PR)
Chaka Fattah (PA)
Ruben Hinojosa (TX)
Carolyn McCarthy (NY)
John Tierney (MA)
Ron Kind (WI)
Loretta Sanchez (CA)
Harold E. Ford, Jr. (TN)
Dennis J. Kucinich (OH)
David Wu (OR)
Rush Holt (NJ)

Minority Staff Director
Gail Weiss
225-3725, 2101 RHOB

House Education and Workforce Subcommittees

Early Childhood, Youth, and Families
225-4527, 2181 RHOB
Republicans: Castle, Chair; Johnson; Souder; Paul; Goodling; Greenwood; McIntosh; Upton; Hilleary; Petri; Roukema; Boehmer; Graham; Schaffer; Salmon; Tancredo; DeMint

Democrats: Kildee, Ranking Member; Miller; Payne; Mink; Scott; Kucinich; Woolsey; Romero-Barcelo; Fattah; Hinojosa; McCarthy; Sanchez; Ford; Wu

Majority Staff Director: Kevin Talley, 225-4527, 2181 RHOB

Minority Staff Director: Gail Weiss, 225-3725, 2101 RHOB

Employer-Employee Relations
225-4527, 2181 RHOB
Republicans: Boehner, Chair; Talent; Petri; Roukema; Ballenger; Goodling; McKeon; Hoekstra; Salmon; Fletcher; DeMint
Democrats: Andrews, Ranking Member; Kildee; Payne; Romero-Barcelo; McCarthy; Tierney; Wu; Holt
Majority Staff Director: Kevin Talley, 225-4527, 2181 RHOB
Minority Staff Director: Gail Weiss, 225-3725, 2101 RHOB

Oversight and Investigations
225-4527, 2181 RHOB
Republicans: Hoekstra, Chair; Norwood; Hilleary; Schaffer; Tancredo; Fletcher
Democrats: Roemer, Ranking Member; Scott; Kind; Ford
Majority Staff Director: Kevin Talley, 225-4527, 2181 RHOB
Minority Staff Director: Gail Weiss, 225-3725, 2101 RHOB

Postsecondary Education, Training, and Life-Long Learning
225-4527, 2181 RHOB
Republicans: McKeon, Chair; Goodling; Petri; Barrett; Greenwood; Graham; McIntosh; Castle; Souder; Deal; Ehlers; Isakson
Democrats: Martinez, Ranking Member; Tierney; Kind; Holt; Owens; Mink; Andrews; Roemer; Fattah; Hinojosa
Majority Staff Director: Kevin Talley, 225-4527, 2181 RHOB
Minority Staff Director: Gail Weiss, 225-3725, 2101 RHOB

Workforce Protections
225-4527, 2181 RHOB
Republicans: Ballenger, Chair; Barrett; Hoekstra; Graham, Paul; Johnson; Boehner; Isakson
Democrats: Owens, Ranking Member; Miller; Martinez; Woolsey; Sanchez; Kucinich
Majority Staff Director: Kevin Talley, 225-4527, 2181 RHOB
Minority Staff Director: Gail Weiss, 225-3725, 2101 RHOB

HOUSE JUDICIARY COMMITTEE
Phone: 225-3951
Room: 2138 RHOB
http://www.house.gov/judiciary

Republicans
Henry J. Hyde (IL), Chair
F. James Sensenbrenner, Jr. (WI)
Bill McCollum (FL)
George W. Gekas (PA)
Howard Coble (NC)
Lamar S. Smith (TX)
Elton Gallegly (CA)
Charles Canady (FL)
Bob Goodlatte (VA)
Steve Buyer (IN)
Ed Bryant (TN)
Steve Chabot (OH)
Bob Barr (GA)
William L. Jenkins (TN)
Asa Hutchinson (AR)
Edward A. Pease (IN)
Christopher Cannon (UT)
James E. Rogan (CA)
Lindsey Graham (SC)
Mary Bono (CA)
Spencer Bachus (AL)

Democrats
John Conyers, Jr. (MI), Ranking Member
Barney Frank (MA)
Howard L. Berman (CA)
Rick Boucher (VA)
Jerrold Nadler (NY)
Robert "Bobby" C. Scott (VA)
Melvin Watt (NC)
Zoe Lofgren (CA)
Sheila Jackson Lee (TX)
Maxine Waters (CA)
Marty Meehan (MA)
William Delahunt (MA)
Robert I. Wexler (FL)
Steven R. Rothman (NJ)
Tammy Baldwin (WI)
Anthony D. Weiner (NY)

Majority Chief of Staff
Tom Mooney, Sr.
225-3951, 2138 RHOB

Minority Chief Counsel/Staff Director
Julian Epstein
225-6504, 2142 RHOB

House Judiciary Subcommittees

Commercial and Administrative Law
225-2835, B-353 RHOB
Republicans: Gekas, Chair; Bryant; Graham; Buyer; Chabot; Hutchinson; Bachus
Democrats: Nadler, Ranking Member; Baldwin; Watt; Weiner; Delahunt

Majority Chief Counsel: Ray Smietanka, 225-2825, B-353 RHOB
Minority Counsel: David Lachmann, 225-2322, B-336 RHOB

Courts and Intellectual Property
225-5741, B-351A RHOB
Republicans: Coble, Chair, Sensenbrenner; Gallegly;
 Goodlatte; Jenkins; Pease; Cannon; Rogan; Bono
Democrats: Berman; Ranking Member; Conyers; Boucher;
 Lofgren; Delahunt; Wexler
Majority Chief Counsel: Mitch Glazier, 225-5741, B-351A
 RHOB
Minority Counsel: Robert Raben, 225-6906, B-351C RHOB

Crime
225-3926, 207 CHOB
Republicans: McCollum, Chair; Buyer; Chabot; Barr; Gekas;
 Coble; Smith; Canady
Democrats: Scott, Ranking Member; Meehan; Rothman;
 Weiner; Jackson Lee
Majority Chief Counsel: Paul McNulty, 225-3926, 207
 CHOB
Minority Counsel: David Yassky, 225-6906, B-336 RHOB

Immigration and Claims
225-5727, B-370B RHOB
Republicans: Smith, Chair; McCollum; Gallegly; Pease;
 Cannon; Bono; Canady; Goodlatte
Democrats: Jackson Lee, Ranking Member; Berman; Lofgren;
 Frank; Meehan
Majority Chief Counsel: George Fishman, 225-5727, B-370B
 RHOB
Minority Counsel: Stephanie Peters, 225-2329, B-351 RHOB

The Constitution
226-7680, H2-362 FHOB
Republicans: Canaday, Chair; Hyde; Hutchinson; Bachus;
 Goodlatte; Barr; Jenkins; Graham
Democrats: Watt, Ranking Member; Waters; Frank;
 Conyers; Nadler
Majority Chief Counsel: John Ladd, 226-7680, H2-362
 FHOB
Minority Counsel: Perry Apelbaum, 225-6504, B-351C
 RHOB

HOUSE RULES COMMITTEE
Phone: 225-9191
Room: H-312 Capitol
http://www.house.gov/rules

Republicans
David Dreier (CA), Chair
Porter J. Goss (FL)
John Linder (GA)
Deborah Pryce (OH)
Lincoln Diaz-Balart (FL)
Doc Hastings (WA)
Sue Myrick (NC)
Pete Sessions (TX)
Tom Reynolds (NY)

Majority Staff Director
Vince Randazzo
225-9191, H-312 Capitol

Democrats
Joe Moakley (MA), Ranking Member
Martin Frost (TX)
Tony P. Hall (OH)
Louise McIntosh Slaughter (NY)

Minority Staff Director
George Crawford
225-9091, H-152 Capitol

House Rules Subcommittees

Rules and Organization of the House
225-8925, 421 CHOB
Republicans: Linder, Chair; Diaz-Balart; Sessions; Reynolds;
 Dreier
Democrats: Hall, Ranking Member; Slaughter
Majority Counsel: Bill Evans, 225-8925, 421 CHOB
Minority Staff Director: Mike Gessel, 225-6465, 1628 LHOB

The Legislative and Budget Process
225-1547, 421 CHOB
Republicans: Goss, Chair; Pryce; Hastings; Myrick; Dreier
Democrats: Frost, Ranking Member; Moakley
Majority Counsel: Merrel Moorehead, 225-1547, 421 CHOB
Minority Staff Director: Kristi Walseth, 225-3605, 2256
 RHOB

HOUSE VETERANS' AFFAIRS COMMITTEE
Phone: 225-3527
Room: 335 CHOB
http://www.house.gov/va

Republicans
Bob Stump (AZ), Chair
Christopher H. Smith (NJ)
Michael Bilirakis (FL)
Floyd Spence (SC)
Terry Everett (AL)
Steve Buyer (IN)

Democrats
Lane Evans (IL), Ranking Member
Bob Filner (CA)
Luis Gutierrez (IL)
Corrine Brown (FL)
Mike Doyle (PA)
Collin Peterson (MN)

Jack Quinn (NY)
Cliff Stearns (FL)
Jerry Moran (KS)
J.D. Hayworth (AZ)
Helen Chenoweth (ID)
Ray LaHood (IL)
James V. Hansen (UT)
Howard McKeon (CA)
James A. Gibbons (NV)
Mike Simpson (ID)
Richard Baker (LA)

Majority Staff Director/Chief Counsel
Carl Commenator
225-3527, 335 CHOB

House Veterans' Affairs Subcommittees

Benefits
225-9164, 337 CHOB
Republicans: Quinn, Chair; Hayworth; LaHood; Hansen;
   Gibbons
Democrats: Filner, Ranking Member; Reyes; Berkley;
   Vacancy
Majority Staff Director: Darryl Kehrer, 225-9164, 337
   CHOB
Minority Staff Director: Jill Cochran, 225-9756, 333 CHOB
Health
225-9154, 338 CHOB
Republicans: Stearns, Chair; Smith; Bilirakis; Bachus; Moran;
   Chenoweth; McKeon; Simpson; Baker

Julia M. Carson (IN)
Silvestre Reyes (TX)
Vic Snyder (AR)
Ciro D. Rodriguez (TX)
Ronnie Shows (MS)
Shelley Berkley (NV)
Vacancy
Vacancy

Minority Staff Director
Michael Durishin
225-9756, 333 CHOB

Democrats: Gutierrez, Ranking Member; Doyle; Peterson;
   Carson; Snyder; Rodriguez; Shows
Majority Staff Director: Ralph Ibson, 225-3527, 338 CHOB
Minority Director: Susan Edgerton, 225-9756, 333 CHOB

Oversight and Investigations
225-9164, 337 CHOB
Republicans: Everett, Chair; Stump; Spence; Buyer
Democrats: Brown, Ranking Member; Vacancy; Vacancy
Majority Staff Director: Kingston Smith, 225-3527, 337 CHOB
Minority Staff Director: Bill Crandel, 225-9756, 333 CHOB

HOUSE WAYS AND MEANS COMMITTEE
Phone: 225-3625
Room: 1102 LHOB
http://www.house.gov/ways_means

Republicans
Bill Archer (TX), Chair
Philip M. Crane (IL)
William M. Thomas (CA)
E. Clay Shaw, Jr. (FL)
Nancy L. Johnson (CT)
Amo Houghton, Jr. (NY)
Wally Herger (CA)
Jim McCrery (LA)
Dave Camp (MI)
Jim Ramstad (MN)
Jim Nussle (IA)
Sam Johnson (TX)
Jennifer Dunn (WA)
Michael "Mac" Collins (GA)
Rob Portman (OH)
Philip S. English (PA)
Wes W. Watkins (OK)
J.D. Hayworth (AZ)
Jerry Weller (IL)
Kenny C. Hulshof (MO)
Scott McInnis (CO)
Ron Lewis (KY)
Mark Foley (FL)

Democrats
Charles B. Rangel (NY), Ranking Member
Fortney Stark (CA)
Robert T. Matsui (CA)
William J. Coyne (PA)
Sander M. Levin (MI)
Benjamin L. Cardin (MD)
Jim McDermott (WA)
Gerald D. Kleczka (WI)
John Lewis (GA)
Richard E. Neal (MA)
Michael R. McNulty (NY)
William J. Jefferson (LA)
John S. Tanner (TN)
Xavier Becerra (CA)
Karen Thurman (FL)
Lloyd Doggett (TX)

Majority Chief of Staff
Pete Singleton
225-3625, 1102 LHOB

House Ways and Means Subcommittees

Health
225-3943, 1136 LHOB
Republicans: Thomas, Chair; Johnson, N.; McCrery; Crane; Johnson, S.; Camp; Ramstad; English
Democrats: Stark, Ranking Member; Kleczka; Lewis; McDermott; Thurman
Majority Staff Director: Ann-Marie Lynch, 225-3943, 1136 LHOB
Minority Professional Staff Member: Bill Vaughan, 225-4021, 1106 LHOB

Human Resources
225-1025, B-317 RHOB
Republicans: Johnson, Chair; English; Watkins; Lewis; Foley; McInnis; McCrery; Camp
Democrats: Cardin, Ranking Member; Stark; Matsui; Coyne; Jefferson
Majority Staff Director: Ron Haskins, 225-1025, B-317 RHOB
Minority Professional Staff Member: Nick Gwyn, 225-4021, 1106 LHOB

Oversight
225-7601, 1136 LHOB
Republicans: Houghton, Chair; Portman; Dunn; Watkins; Weller; Hulshof; Hayworth; McInnis

Minority Chief Counsel
Janice Mays
225-4021, 1106 LHOB

Democrats: Coyne, Ranking Member; McNulty; McDermott; Lewis; Neal
Majority Staff Director: William "Mac" McKenney, 225-7601, 1136 LHOB
Minority Counsel: Beth Vance, 225-4021, 1106 LHOB

Social Security
225-9263, B-316 RHOB
Republicans: Shaw, Chair; Johnson, S.; Collins; Portman; Hayworth; Weller; Hulshof; McCrery
Democrats: Matsui, Ranking Member; Levin; Tanner; Doggett; Cardin
Majority Staff Director: Kim Hildred, 225-9263, B-316 RHOB
Minority Counsel: Sandy Wise, 225-4021, 1106 LHOB

Trade
225-6649, 1104 LHOB
Republicans: Crane, Chair; Thomas; Shaw; Houghton; Camp; Ramstad; Dunn; Herger; Nussle
Democrats: Levin, Ranking Member; Rangel; Neal; McNulty; Jefferson; Becerra
Majority Staff Director: Thelma Askey, 225-6649, 1104 LHOB
Minority Counsel: Tim Reif, 225-4021, 1106 LHOB